STUDENT UNIT GUIDE

NEW EDITION

AQA AS Law Unit I
Law Making and the Legal System

Peter Darwent and Ian Yule

PHILIP ALLAN

Philip Allan Updates, an imprint of Hodder Education, an Hachette UK company, Market Place, Deddington, Oxfordshire OX15 0SE

Orders

Bookpoint Ltd, 130 Milton Park, Abingdon, Oxfordshire OX14 4SB
tel: 01235 827827
fax: 01235 400401
e-mail: education@bookpoint.co.uk
Lines are open 9.00 a.m.–5.00 p.m., Monday to Saturday, with a 24-hour message answering service. You can also order through the Philip Allan Updates website: www.philipallan.co.uk

ISBN 978-1-4441-7188-4

First printed 2012
Impression number 5 4 3 2 1
Year 2016 2015 2014 2013 2012

Cover photo: blas/Fotolia

Typeset by Integra Software Services Pvt. Ltd., Pondicherry, India

Printed in Dubai

Hachette UK's policy is to use papers that are natural, renewable and recyclable products and made from wood grown in sustainable forests. The logging and manufacturing processes are expected to conform to the environmental regulations of the country of origin.

P2086

Contents

Getting the most from this book

Questions & Answers

Exam-style questions

Examiner comments on the questions
Tips on what you need to do to gain full marks, indicated by the icon ℮.

Sample student answers
Practise the questions, then look at the student answers that follow each set of questions.

Examiner commentary on sample student answers
Find out how many marks each answer would be awarded in the exam and read the examiner comments (preceded by the icon ℮) following each student answer.

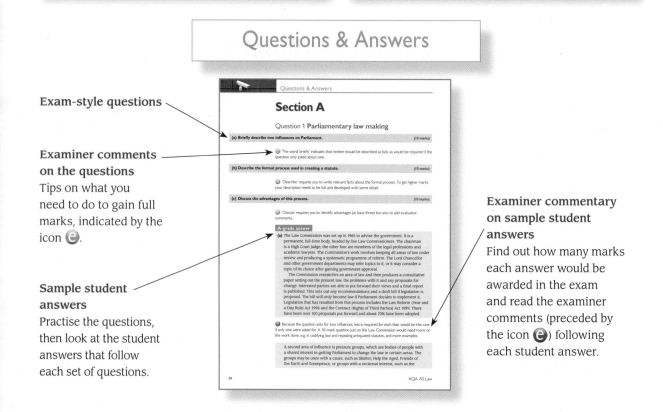

Questions & Answers

Section A

Question 1 **Parliamentary law making**

(a) Briefly describe two influences on Parliament. (10 marks)

℮ The word 'briefly' indicates that neither should be described as fully as would be required if the question only asked about one.

(b) Describe the formal process used in creating a statute. (10 marks)

℮ 'Describe' requires you to write relevant facts about the formal process. To get higher marks your description needs to be full and developed with some detail.

(c) Discuss the advantages of this process. (10 marks)

℮ 'Discuss' requires you to identify advantages (at least three) but also to add evaluative comments.

A-grade answer

(a) The Law Commission was set up in 1965 to advise the government. It is a permanent, full-time body, headed by five Law Commissioners. The chairman is a High Court judge; the other four are members of the legal professions and academic lawyers. The Commission's work involves keeping all areas of law under review and producing a systematic programme of reform. The Lord Chancellor and other government departments may refer topics to it, or it may consider a topic of its choice after gaining government approval.

The Commission researches an area of law and then produces a consultative paper setting out the present law, the problems with it and any proposals for change. Interested parties are able to put forward their views and a final report is published. This sets out any recommendations and a draft bill if legislation is proposed. The bill will only become law if Parliament decides to implement it. Legislation that has resulted from this process includes the Law Reform (Year and a Day Rule) Act 1996 and the Contract (Rights of Third Parties) Act 1999. There have been over 100 proposals put forward and about 70% have been adopted.

℮ Because the question asks for two influences, less is required for each than would be the case if only one were asked for. A 10-mark question just on the Law Commission would need more on the work done, e.g. in codifying law and repealing antiquated statutes, and more examples.

A second area of influence is pressure groups, which are bodies of people with a shared interest in getting Parliament to change the law in certain areas. The groups may be ones with a cause, such as Shelter, Help the Aged, Friends of the Earth and Greenpeace, or groups with a sectional interest, such as the

84   AQA AS Law

About this book

The AQA specification for the AS and A2 Law examinations is divided into four units. AS Unit 1 deals with **law making** and **the legal system**. The topics within this part of the specification are designed to provide a sound introduction to the way the English legal system works; they cover the different types of court and the alternatives to courts, lawyers, judges, the particular importance of lay people, and the ways in which access to justice is ensured.

There are two sections to this guide:

- **Content Guidance** — this sets out the specification content for Unit 1, breaking it down into manageable sections for study and learning. It also contains references to cases that you need to study for a sound understanding of each topic.
- **Questions and Answers** — this provides nine sample AS questions. Each question is followed by an A-grade answer. Examiner's comments show how marks are awarded.

Content Guidance

Section A: Law making

Parliamentary law making

UK legislation consists of Acts of Parliament, which are also known as statutes. It is the result of a process involving the House of Commons, the House of Lords and the monarch (the queen). Statutes are referred to as **primary legislation**. Most legislation is drawn up (drafted) by the government.

The House of Commons is made up of Members of Parliament (MPs), elected to represent the people in their individual local constituencies. The political party that has the majority of seats forms the government of the day. The House of Lords, which is unelected, consists (at the time of writing) of 91 hereditary peers, with the rest of the House being life peers appointed by the government, Law Lords and senior bishops.

How statutes are created

All Acts of Parliament begin life as bills, of which there are two types: public bills and private bills.

Public bills

Public bills are by far the most common and they can be subdivided into government bills and private members' bills.

Government bills are introduced and piloted through the parliamentary process by a government minister. Some are controversial and reflect the views of the political party in power, such as the bills to privatise public utilities under the Conservative governments of Margaret Thatcher and John Major; others are concerned simply with the smooth running of the country, such as the **Access to Justice Act 1999**. There are some 40 to 50 government bills each year, most of which become law.

Before a bill is drawn up, the government department involved in the proposed changes to the law may issue a consultative document known as a **Green Paper**, setting out the proposals and allowing interested parties to comment on them. Any necessary changes can then be made and the final proposals set out in a **White Paper**. For example, the **Court and Legal Services Act 1990** was preceded by three Green Papers published in January 1989 and a White Paper ('Legal services: a framework for the future') published in July 1989, which set out the then government's proposals in relation to legal services generally. The bill is drawn up by parliamentary counsel, specialist lawyers in drafting bills, on the instructions of the relevant government department.

Private members' bills are introduced by backbench MPs, whose names have been selected by ballot (20 each year). The choice of subject is their own but, as time for debate on these bills is limited, few become law. Success rates vary considerably from year to year. For example, in the 1996–97 session 26% of private members' bills were successful, whereas in 2002–03 just 13% were. In 2000–01, none reached the Statute Book.

To be successful, a private member's bill needs to have the tacit support of the government of the day. A good example is the **Abortion Act 1967**, which resulted from David Steel's private member's bill and with which the Labour government sympathised. Other examples of private member's bills that have become law include the **Murder (Abolition of Death Penalty) Act 1965**, the **Marriage Act 1994**, which allowed buildings other than register offices or places of worship to be used to conduct marriages, and the **Computer Misuse Act 1990**.

Private bills

Private bills are usually put forward by a local authority, public corporation or large public company and only affect the bodies concerned. A recent example is the **Medway Council Act 2004**, which gave Medway Council more power to control street trading in the borough.

There are also hybrid bills, which, when they become statutes, alter the general law but particularly affect the legal rights of a small number of people. The **Channel Tunnel Act 1987** and the **Crossrail Act 2008** are good examples. In both cases major transport projects would have significant impact on local people.

Process of a bill through Parliament

A bill cannot become an Act of Parliament until it has been passed by both Houses of Parliament. The procedure consists of a number of stages and may commence in either the House of Commons or the House of Lords, although finance bills must begin in the House of Commons.

First reading

This takes place when the title of the bill is read out to the House.

Second reading

This crucial stage allows the House to hold a full debate on the main principles of the bill. At the end of the debate, a vote is taken as to whether the bill should proceed further.

Committee stage

If the vote is in favour, the bill passes to the committee stage. This involves a detailed examination of each clause of the bill by a standing committee of between 16 and

Knowledge check 1

Roughly how many government bills are there each year?

Knowledge check 2

What is a private member's bill?

50 MPs. They will probably propose amendments to various clauses of the bill. Some amendments are put forward by opponents of the bill and are often politically motivated, but many are of a technical nature, designed to improve the bill.

Report stage

The committee reports back to the House on any amendments that have been made. These are debated and voted on.

Third reading

The bill is presented again to the House and the final vote is taken.

Passage through the other House

If the bill was introduced in the House of Commons, it then passes to the House of Lords (or vice versa), where the same procedure is repeated. If the House of Lords makes amendments to a bill that has already passed through the House of Commons, the bill is referred back to the Commons to consider the amendments.

Royal assent

Once a bill has passed successfully through all the stages in both Houses, it has to receive formal consent of the monarch in order to become law. This is known as royal assent.

Some Acts of Parliament come into force when royal assent is given, but most start on a specific date, which may be stated in the Act. Sometimes, different parts of the Act may come into effect at different times, which can cause uncertainty, as it can be difficult to find out which sections are in force.

Usually the legislative process takes several months to complete, especially if the proposals are controversial. On some occasions, however, if all the parties agree that a new law is needed urgently, an Act may be passed in 24 hours, such as the **Northern Ireland Bill 1972**.

Role of the House of Commons

Because the House of Commons is the elected body, it has the most important role in the law-making process. All important legislation begins in the House of Commons and all finance bills must start there.

By using the Parliament Acts, the Commons can defeat any attempt by the Lords to oppose a measure that the Commons has passed. In practice, this power is rarely used and the Commons often has to compromise in order to get legislation through. Because the Lords can delay a bill for a year, it has considerably more influence over the Commons during the last year of a Parliament's life.

In practice, any bill that the Commons passes will be either a government bill or a private member's bill that the government supports. The House of Commons is therefore not a truly independent body. In most cases, it does what the government tells it to do, because a majority of MPs are members of the governing party and pressured by the whips into supporting government bills.

Knowledge check 3

(a) What is the crucial stage in the passage of a bill?

(b) What happens in it?

Examiner tip

In a question asking about the formal process of law making or the stages through which a bill passes you should deal separately with the process in each House and draw attention to the power that the Commons has under the Parliament Acts to force through legislation.

Role of the House of Lords

Bills can start life in the House of Lords, though most begin in the Commons. Usually the legislation that starts in the Lords is not politically controversial or has a legal subject matter, for example the **Access to Justice Act 1999**. Occasionally, more controversial legislation can start in the House of Lords. This happened with the **Human Rights Act 1998**, which was introduced for the government by the Lord Chancellor, who was a peer rather than an MP. A recent Act that started in the Lords is the **Academies Act 2010**, which enables all state schools to apply for academy status.

However, the House of Lords is primarily a revising and debating chamber, and it allows further detailed scrutiny of bills that have already passed through the House of Commons.

At times, the House of Lords has made the government rethink its proposals. For example, in March 2005 it forced the government to amend its plans in the **Terrorism Bill** for control orders to deal with terrorist suspects.

The unelected House of Lords used to be able to prevent legislation put forward by the elected House of Commons, as the agreement of both Houses was necessary. This power is restricted by the **Parliament Acts 1911 and 1949**. If the House of Lords rejects a bill, it can still become law, provided it is reintroduced to the House of Commons in the next parliamentary session and passes all the stages again. The Lords are not allowed to delay finance bills.

This power to force the Lords to pass a bill has only been used five times — for example to push through the **War Crimes Act 1991** and the **Hunting Act 2004**.

Usually, a government threat to use the Parliament Acts is enough. Initially, the Lords rejected the lowering of the homosexual age of consent from 18 to 16 when this was introduced as part of the **Crime and Disorder Bill 1998**, but in 2000 a new bill was introduced, and after the government made it clear that it would invoke the Parliament Acts, the House of Lords gave in.

> **Knowledge check 4**
> How many times have the Parliament Acts been used to force through legislation?

Role of the Crown

The Crown plays a purely formal role, and any attempt by a monarch to thwart the will of the Commons and Lords would not be tolerated. Since Queen Anne refused to pass the **Scotch Militia Bill 1707**, no monarch has refused to assent to a bill.

Advantages of the UK law-making system

- The House of Commons is an elected body. MPs are answerable to the voters and there must be an election at least every 5 years. The Commons can, if necessary, force its will on the Lords by using the Parliament Acts.
- Parliament takes note of public opinion. While a bill is going through Parliament, there are opportunities for people to lobby and express their views. The decision of the House of Commons in February 2006 to vote for a complete ban on smoking in public places could be seen as Parliament responding to public opinion.
- The House of Lords is not elected, so it is less concerned with staying popular with voters. It can therefore be a useful check on a government that has a large majority

> **Examiner tip**
> Notice that while the role of the Crown is purely formal and should be mentioned quite briefly in any answer, the House of Lords has a number of roles and should be discussed in more detail. However, the role of the Commons should be emphasised as the most important.

in the Commons. For example, in January 2012 the Lords tried to make changes to the **Welfare Reform Bill**, reflecting concerns that some aspects of the bill will create real hardship.

- There are many people in the Lords who have specialist expertise, for example lawyers, doctors and scientists, or who have been successful in running companies or charities. These people bring practical knowledge and experience to their examination of bills.
- The legislative process is thorough, with detailed committee examination of bills in both Houses as well as general debates.
- Delegated legislation means that much of the detail can be left to government departments to draw up through statutory instruments.
- When it is necessary, an Act can be passed quickly. For example, the **Criminal Justice (Terrorism and Conspiracy) Act 1998** went through all its stages in 2 days, and the **Northern Ireland Act 1972** was passed in just 24 hours.

Examiner tip

When dealing with advantages or disadvantages, you should try to refer to some examples and explain why each particular point is an advantage or disadvantage.

Disadvantages of the UK law-making system

- There is not enough time to pass all the legislation that is necessary, and reform bills (e.g. to modernise the law on non-fatal offences) are often left out of the government's legislative programme.
- Because the government usually has a comfortable majority in the Commons, it is difficult for Parliament to influence or change what the government wants. For example, several aspects of the **Criminal Justice and Public Order Act 1994** were criticised, yet no changes were made during its passage through Parliament. Also, although the Lords inflicted seven defeats on the **Welfare Reform Bill** in January 2012, these were immediately reversed in the Commons, and it seems likely that the government will get its proposals into law.
- There is inadequate scrutiny of legislation. The government controls the parliamentary timetable, and through processes such as the guillotine it can restrict discussion of a bill. Also, because the government has a majority on all the standing committees, it is able to defeat any amendments put forward in committee. H. W. R. Wade argues that 'the most shocking feature of our legislative process is the way in which parliamentary scrutiny is eliminated on the pretext of shortage of time'.
- Some bills are passed too quickly, usually in response to a real or imagined emergency. The **Dangerous Dogs Act 1991** was described by a judge in one case as bearing 'all the hallmarks of an ill-thought-out piece of legislation, no doubt in hasty response to yet another strident pressure group'.
- The House of Lords, which is not elected, is able to delay legislation that the House of Commons has passed. No other democratic country has an unelected second chamber able to frustrate the decisions of an elected body in this way.
- The original proposals in a bill can be amended, often more than once. This can result in the final legislation being unclear in some areas and having to be interpreted later by the courts.

Doctrine of parliamentary supremacy

Parliamentary supremacy (sovereignty) is a fundamental part of the UK constitution. It means that as a democratically elected body, Parliament is the supreme law-making body in the country. A. V. Dicey, the nineteenth-century jurist, stated: 'Parliament has the right to make or unmake any law whatever; and, further…no person or body is recognised by the law of England as having a right to override or set aside the legislation of Parliament.' In practice, it means that Acts of Parliament passed using the proper procedures cannot be challenged. They must be applied by the courts and override any judicial precedent, delegated legislation or previous Act of Parliament that covers that area of law. Parliament also has the power to rescind (unmake) any law it has passed.

Another aspect is the idea that no Parliament can bind its successors (i.e. no Parliament can make laws that will restrict law making in future Parliaments). Acts of Parliament can also apply retrospectively (i.e. to past events) and extra-territorially (i.e. to events outside the UK). An Act combining both these elements was the **War Crimes Act 1991**, which allowed the prosecution of people for crimes committed in Europe during the Second World War.

Examiner tip
Note that a question might refer to either the sovereignty or the supremacy of Parliament. You would answer questions on each in the same way — first explaining what the term means and then identifying the characteristics that illustrate it.

Limitations on sovereignty

Public opinion

There have always been practical limits to what Parliament can do. All politicians are sensitive to public opinion and plans for law making are likely to reflect this.

Entrenched laws

There are entrenched laws, which deal with fundamental constitutional issues and which would be difficult for any future Parliament to change, for example legislation extending voting rights to women and lowering the voting age to 18. Another example is the more recent granting of legislative powers to a Scottish Parliament.

Membership of the European Union (EU)

Under the Treaty of Rome 1957, European Community law, enacted by the powers set out in treaties, takes priority over conflicting laws in member states. (To become binding, treaties have to be ratified by all member states, and at the time of writing it is uncertain whether the Treaty of Lisbon will come into effect after its rejection by Ireland in a referendum in June 2008.) The **European Communities Act 1972** incorporates this principle into UK law. Even if Parliament passes an Act that conflicts with EU law, EU law must prevail, as shown in the *Factortame* case in 1990. For areas of law not covered by the EU, Parliament is supreme.

Human Rights Act 1998

This came into force in October 2000 and incorporates the European Convention on Human Rights into English law. Under the Act, the Convention does not have superiority over English law and Parliament can still make laws that conflict with it. However, under s.19 of the Act, all bills require a statement from a government minister before the second reading in each House, saying that the provisions of the bill are compatible with the Convention or, if not, that the government nevertheless intends the bill to proceed.

Under s.3 of the Act, the courts are required as far as possible to interpret Acts so that they comply with the Convention. If an Act cannot be reconciled with the Convention, a judge can make a declaration of incompatibility, although ministers are not obliged to change the law. It could be argued that because Parliament can refuse to respond to a declaration by a judge that an Act is incompatible with the Convention, the doctrine of parliamentary supremacy is unaffected. However, it is clearly significant that judges can challenge the validity of Acts of Parliament, and in practice it is likely that a government will accept that the legislation has to change. For example, in 2001 the **Mental Health Act 1983** was amended following a declaration of incompatibility in *H* v *Mental Health Review Tribunal* (2001).

Influences on Parliament

In order to be effective, the law must be able to adapt to changes in society, so the law-making process has to be ongoing. There are many pressures on Parliament that try to influence the direction of this process, ranging from political considerations such as the party manifesto to law reform agencies or other pressure/interest groups.

Political pressures

When a general election is to be held, each political party presents a **party manifesto**, setting out its proposals for new legislation if elected into government. These have covered such things as the right to buy council houses, included in the Conservative Party's 1979 manifesto and implemented through the **Housing Act 1980**. The **Human Rights Act 1998**, which implemented the Labour Party's manifesto commitment to incorporate the European Convention on Human Rights into English law, and the **House of Lords Act 1999**, which greatly reduced the number of hereditary peers, were also the result of manifesto commitments.

Some bills are responses to particular and unexpected events, such as the **Prevention of Terrorism (Temporary Provisions) Act 1974** in response to the Birmingham IRA bombings, and the **Drought Act 1976**, which was introduced to deal with a serious drought in the summer of 1976.

Membership of the EU is another influence, as it creates obligations under the treaties whereby decisions made by the EU Commission or Council of Ministers must be enacted as new laws. For example, the **Consumer Protection Act 1987** was passed to give effect to the Product Liability Directive, which imposes strict liability on producers for damage caused by their products.

The civil service in each ministerial department also has its own views as to the legislation necessary to achieve its goals.

Advantages of political influences

- Governments are elected and they usually respond to what the public wants. They wish to be re-elected, so it is unlikely they will pass unpopular Acts.
- It is helpful that when there is an emergency, the government can respond quickly and use its influence over Parliament to pass appropriate emergency measures. The **Anti-terrorism, Crime and Security Act 2001** is an example.

- Parliament is also flexible enough to respond to other political influences. Individual MPs have been responsible for valuable reforms, such as the abolition of the death penalty and the regulation of minicabs in London.
- Governmental ideas for legislation are thought out and planned with the help of expert civil servants. The civil servants have to implement the new laws, so it is likely that they will have thought about any problems.

Disadvantages of political influences

- Governments want to be popular, so they are reluctant to introduce laws that are necessary but unpopular, such as tougher rules on speeding or on drinking and driving.
- Because they are concerned with being re-elected, governments concentrate on passing laws that will make them popular. As a result, necessary but non-urgent law reforms, such as improving the law on non-fatal offences, are neglected.
- The government usually gets its way if it has a large majority in the House of Commons. This can give the impression that Parliament is weak and largely ineffective in modifying government proposals.

Examiner tip

When discussing an influence on Parliament you should explain the importance of it for law making. This is best done by referring to examples of actual statutes.

Pressure groups

Pressure groups are bodies of people with a shared interest in getting the government to change the law in certain areas. They include groups such as Shelter, Help the Aged, Greenpeace, Friends of the Earth, trade unions, business groups such as the Confederation of British Industry and professional organisations such as the Law Society.

They target politicians, civil servants and local government offices by lobbying MPs, organising petitions and gaining as much publicity as possible for their cause. Well-organised groups, such as Greenpeace and Friends of the Earth, have been successful. Governments now have to consider the environmental impact of their policies because of heightened public awareness of environmental issues. Shelter was successful in persuading the government to introduce change for homeless people in the **Housing Homeless Persons Act 1977**. At times, groups may join forces to get their point across to the government. This happened when people opposed to the banning of fox hunting held a joint march in London with the Countryside Alliance.

Large groups are often more successful than smaller ones, but sometimes one person can bring about change almost single-handedly. The late Mary Whitehouse headed a campaign against child pornography, which led the government to introduce the **Protection of Children Act 1984**.

Some pressure groups exist only for a short time, as they are set up to deal with a specific issue, for instance a campaign about a proposed bypass. The group disbands once the issue is resolved. An example is the National Campaign for the Abolition of Capital Punishment, which was set up in 1955 and disbanded in 1969 when the suspension of the death penalty was made permanent.

Sometimes a pressure group is set up as a result of a tragic event. The Snowdrop Campaign, organised after the Dunblane massacre in 1996, resulted in Parliament banning the private ownership of most types of handgun.

Sectional or interest groups exist to further the ends of their own particular section of society. Examples are trade unions, groups such as the National Farmers' Union (NFU) or the Confederation of British Industry (CBI), and professional associations such as the British Medical Association and the Law Society.

The degree of influence exercised by such groups varies. Trade unions traditionally have more power under Labour governments, while their importance declined sharply during the Conservative governments from 1979 to 1997. Groups such as the CBI and the NFU would expect to be consulted by governments of all political persuasions, though traditionally they have more influence under Conservative governments.

Professional associations representing groups such as lawyers and doctors, made up of well-educated, articulate and often wealthy individuals, are influential, and governments of all parties would tend to consult them before introducing a bill affecting their interests. For example, the Law Society, which represents solicitors, has a parliamentary unit that actively lobbies MPs and peers from all parties for changes in the law. The ban on smoking in public places in July 2007 was partly the result of lobbying by the British Medical Association (BMA).

Knowledge check 5

What are pressure groups?

Advantages of pressure groups

- Pressure groups give the public and particularly minorities a voice. They act as a safety valve for frustrations, as in pro-hunting and anti-Iraq War protests.
- They help MPs keep in touch with what people think. For example, pressure from environmental groups may have persuaded the government to change car tax regulations to favour smaller, more fuel-efficient cars and pressure from the BMA helped to persuade the government to introduce the ban on smoking in public places in 2007.
- They raise public awareness of issues that affect their interest or cause. For example, Fathers 4 Justice has been successful through a variety of stunts in raising awareness of the plight of many fathers denied access to their children after a divorce.
- Members of pressure groups often have considerable expertise and can therefore suggest detailed and well-thought-out law changes. Many groups have draft bills ready for backbench MPs to introduce.

Disadvantages of pressure groups

- Some large pressure groups that represent powerful organisations are extremely influential, and it is difficult for smaller pressure groups to match their influence. Environmental groups claim that the strength of the road lobby and the airline industry means that new roads or airport extensions are difficult to fight.
- The methods of some pressure groups can be a problem, for example strikes and protests can cause disruption, such as the blockading of oil depots. The direct-action tactics of Fathers 4 Justice have been criticised. Members of the Countryside Alliance broke into the House of Commons as part of its campaign in favour of fox hunting. Extremist groups, such as animal rights activists, may even break the law by attacking scientific laboratories and the homes and property of individual employees of drug companies.
- Even if an interest or pressure group does manage to present its arguments, this does not mean that its views will be taken into consideration.

Examiner tip

Questions on influences will sometimes allow you to choose which one you want to talk about, but they may also specify particular influences, so you need to be prepared for this.

The media

The media include television, radio, newspapers and journals, and they play a powerful role in bringing issues to the attention of the government. Newspapers in particular promote specific issues or causes. For example, the *Daily Mail* has often run headlines on immigration or asylum issues in order to try to achieve tighter controls, and the *Sun* has consistently campaigned against what it sees as the growing influence of the EU on British life. Another example of media influence was the campaign run by the *News of the World* in 2000 following the murder of Sarah Payne by a paedophile. It published details of known paedophiles in order to force the government to take action. The result was a register of sex offenders and the promise of much closer supervision of those released into the community.

Advantages of the media

- The media play a powerful role in bringing issues to the attention of Parliament or the government and can force them to act. A good example is the publication in 2009 of MPs' expenses claims by the *Daily Telegraph*. This led to the reform of the whole system.
- Coverage in newspapers and on television and radio can raise the public profile of an issue and add weight to public opinion.

Disadvantages of the media

- It is a concern that ownership of British newspapers and other branches of the media is in the hands of a relatively small number of individuals. Newspapers often adopt views that reflect those of their owners. Rupert Murdoch, who owns the *Sun*, *The Times*, the *Sunday Times* and Sky television, has used his newspapers to project his own views, particularly his strong opposition to the EU. It remains to be seen whether changes will be made as a result of the Leveson Inquiry into press behaviour which might restrict the influence of the press.
- Concern has also been expressed about links between the media and politicians. The appointment of Andy Coulson, the former *News of the World* editor, as David Cameron's director of communications between 2007 and 2011 was particularly controversial and highlighted fears that the relationship between politicians and the Murdoch-owned media was too cosy. The phone hacking scandal led to Mr Coulson's resignation in January 2011.
- The media have a tendency to create panics by drawing attention to and often exaggerating issues, such as the activities of paedophiles. In some cases, the media whip up public opinion instead of reflecting it.

Examiner tip
There may be developments in this area after this book has gone to press. Remember that you should follow events in the news and be prepared to add new material to an exam answer.

The Law Commission

This was established by the **Law Commission Act 1965**. It is a full-time body with five Commissioners. The chairperson is a High Court judge and the other four are from the legal professions and academic lawyers. Their members of staff are all legally trained. The Commission's work involves looking at reform of the law, codification and consolidation.

The Commission may have topics referred to it by the Lord Chancellor and government departments, or may select a topic of its own, which will be considered after government approval has been gained.

After researching a selected area of law, the Commission produces a consultative paper that details the present law, setting out the problems and options for change. The views of interested parties are sought, after which a final report is published, setting out recommendations and, if legislation is proposed, a draft bill. This will only become law if it goes through the full parliamentary process. Legislation that has resulted from this process includes the **Law Reform (Year and a Day Rule) Act 1996** and the **Contract (Rights of Third Parties) Act 1999**.

The success of the Law Commission in achieving law reform has varied. Initially, there was a high success rate in getting its proposals accepted and enacted, but this has not been maintained. During 1994–95, improvements were brought about by the introduction of new parliamentary procedures. However, in recent years the backlog of proposals has increased again. In 2003–04, the Law Commission reported that seven proposals had been made law, but a further 17 were awaiting parliamentary time and 13 were waiting for a government decision. In 2006 the Law Commission proposed a major reform of the law on murder. The government made a partial response and adopted some of the proposals on voluntary manslaughter in the **Coroner's and Justice Act 2009**, but it did not adopt the more radical idea of introducing two degrees of murder.

Another aim of the Law Commission is to codify the law in certain areas, but this has not been achieved. The Draft Criminal Code was published in 1985 but has never become law. The arguments in favour of codification are that it would make the law accessible and understandable, and provide consistency and certainty. People would be able to know what the law is as it would be contained in one place. The arguments against codification are that a detailed code would make the law too rigid, but if it is insufficiently detailed it will need to be interpreted by the courts, creating uncertainty. Therefore, the Commission has selected areas of law and clarified them, hoping to codify them at a later date if possible. The **Land Registration Act 2002** and the **Fraud Act 2006** are examples of areas of law reformed in this way.

Consolidation involves drawing together all the provisions set out in a number of statutes, so that they are all in one Act. About five consolidation bills are produced each year. A problem with this is that even when the area of law is consolidated, further Acts of Parliament can change it again. The **Powers of the Criminal Courts (Sentencing) Act 2000** was changed by the **Criminal Justice and Courts Act 2000**, where community sentences were renamed and new powers of sentencing created.

Advantages of the Law Commission

- It is made up of lawyers with much expertise, headed by a High Court judge. The Commissioners change every 5 years, so a different range of views is brought into the law-reform process.
- It is a permanent, full-time body and can investigate any areas of law it thinks needs to be reformed.

Knowledge check 6

(a) When was the Law Commission established?

(b) Give an example of a piece of legislation that has resulted from its work.

- It produces draft bills ready for Parliament to introduce, which reduces the workload for ministers.
- It has been responsible for many sensible changes to the law, for example the **Unfair Contract Terms Act 1977**, the **Fraud Act 2006** and the abolition of the 'Year and a Day' rule.
- It can undertake extensive research and engage in wide consultation, so its recommendations for law reform are well informed and this helps to avoid problems in the application of the law.

Disadvantages of the Law Commission

- Parliament has often ignored the Commission's proposals. Up until 1999, only two-thirds of its proposals had been implemented. Often this is because governments cannot find time in the legislative programme for non-urgent law reform. A good example is reform of the law on non-fatal offences. This was recommended by the Law Commission in a report in 1993 and accepted by the new Labour government which even produced a draft bill in 1998, but the government did not proceed with this.
- Sometimes, because its recommendations are usually balanced and measured, they may not suit the political agenda of the government of the day.
- The Law Commission investigates as many as 20–30 areas at the same time. This may mean that each investigation is not as thorough as one carried out by a Royal Commission or a Commission of Inquiry.

Examiner tip
If you are asked about advantages or disadvantages of influences, you should try to explain why each particular point is an advantage or disadvantage and also try to refer to some evidence/examples.

Summary

There are two different types of bill:
- public bills which include government bills (the most important) and private members' bills
- private bills

The process of a bill through Parliament involves both formal and informal processes:
- informal process: consultation and lobbying, Green and White Papers
- formal process: first reading, second reading, committee stage, report stage, third reading; stages repeated in the other House; royal assent

The role of the Commons/Lords/Crown:
- The Commons is the most important: it is an elected body and can force legislation through even if the Lords objects.
- The Lords has important roles and many bills start life there, but Parliament Acts have been used five times by the Commons to pass bills the Lords opposed.
- The Crown has a purely formal role.

Advantages of the UK law-making system include:
- the elected body can impose its will on the Lords
- Parliament takes note of public opinion
- the Lords is a useful check on a government with a large majority

Disadvantages of the process include:
- inadequate scrutiny of legislation
- the government has too much power
- the House of Lords is unelected

Parliamentary sovereignty: Parliament is the supreme law-making body, but there are limitations, e.g. it is subject to EU rules and decisions and is restrained by the Human Rights Act.

Influences on Parliament:
- political influences, e.g. party manifestos and EU decisions
- pressure groups of many different kinds: they use a variety of methods to influence, e.g. demonstrations or lobbying; some pressure groups have more access to government than others
- the media, particularly television and the press
- the Law Commission, which has the specific task of recommending reforms to the law

Delegated legislation

Delegated legislation (secondary legislation) is law that is not made by Parliament but that has its authority. Parliament, in many cases in a statute, may create a framework of law. Authority (permission) is usually given in a 'parent' Act of Parliament known as an **enabling Act**. This Act creates the framework of the law and then delegates power to others to make more detailed law in that area. Examples of enabling Acts are the **Local Government Act 1972**, which allows local authorities such as district and county councils to make bylaws, and the **Access to Justice Act 1999**, which gives the Lord Chancellor wide powers to alter aspects of the system of state funding for legal cases.

Types of delegated legislation

Orders in Council

Orders in Council are made by the Privy Council and can be used for a wide variety of purposes, for example the regulation of certain professional bodies. They are used when an ordinary statutory instrument would be inappropriate, for instance when transferring responsibilities between government departments. Orders in Council were used to transfer powers from ministers of the UK government to ministers of the devolved assemblies in Scotland and Wales. They are used to dissolve Parliament in preparation for a general election and sometimes to make specific law changes as under the **Misuse of Drugs Act 1971** to reclassify cannabis. They are also used to give effect to European directives under s.2(2) of the **European Communities Act 1972**.

In times of emergency, when Parliament is not sitting, the queen and Privy Council may make an Order in Council under the **Emergency Powers Act 1920** and the **Civil Contingencies Act 2004**. These powers were used during the foot-and-mouth crisis in 2001, when decisions needed to be made quickly to try to prevent the spread of the disease. They were also used during the fuel crisis of 2000.

Statutory instruments

This is the most common type of delegated legislation. There were 3,662 statutory instruments made in 2007. Authority is given to ministers and government departments to make these regulations for their area of responsibility, for example the Minister of Transport has the power under various Road Traffic Acts to make detailed road traffic regulations. Under the **Road Traffic Act 1998** the **Traffic Signs Regulations 2002** were made which regulate the size and colour of road signs.

Regulations are a good way of updating primary legislation and adapting the law to changing circumstances. For example, the **Health and Safety at Work Act 1974** has been updated through the **Management of Health and Safety at Work Regulations 1992**.

Statutory instruments are used to implement European Union directives in English law. An example is the **Unfair Terms in Consumer Contracts Regulations 1994**, which implemented a directive aimed at giving greater protection to consumers.

Examiner tip

You should always expect to be asked to describe at least one type of delegated legislation. Often the type(s) will be specified. You need to be confident that you can describe all three types, with suitable examples.

Knowledge check 7

What are Orders in Council?

They are also used to bring an Act of Parliament, or parts of it, into effect by means of a Commencement Order. For example, the **Equality Act 2010** was brought into effect in stages by five Commencement Orders.

Bylaws

Parliament has given local authorities and other public bodies the right to make law in certain areas. Local authorities, such as county councils, district councils and parish councils, can make bylaws to cover such things as parking restrictions and banning the drinking of alcohol in certain public places. Under s.19 of the **Public Libraries and Museums Act 1964** Cornwall County Council made bylaws about the use of libraries in the county. The introduction of the congestion charge zone in central London is another example.

Public corporations and certain companies can also make bylaws to help to enforce rules concerning public behaviour. The London Underground's ban on smoking is an example of this. Another example is the **National Trust Act 1907**, under which the National Trust has power to make bylaws affecting National Trust property. All bylaws must be approved by the relevant government minister.

Professional regulations

Professional regulations also come under the heading of delegated legislation, such as those found in the **Solicitors Act 1974** empowering the Law Society to regulate the conduct of its members.

Control of delegated legislation

Why do we need controls over delegated legislation?

Statistically, there is far more delegated legislation made per year than primary legislation. A great deal of legislation is therefore being made by persons and bodies other than Parliament, without being subject to the full scrutiny of the parliamentary process.

Because most delegated legislation is not made by elected bodies and many people have the power to create it, it is important to make sure that the power is not abused and is controlled. This can be done by Parliament or the courts.

Control by Parliament

Parliament has some control at the time an enabling Act is made, as it sets the limits for making delegated legislation under that Act.

In addition, the Delegated Powers Scrutiny Committee in the House of Lords can decide whether the provisions in a bill to delegate legislative power are inappropriate. Its report is presented to the House of Lords before the committee stage but it has no power to amend the bill.

Knowledge check 8

What are statutory instruments?

Knowledge check 9

What are bylaws?

Examiner tip

It is a good idea to have examples of bylaws from your local area which you can use in your exam answers.

Examiner tip

Students often confuse parliamentary and judicial controls and write about the wrong one in the exam. Parliamentary controls are those which Parliament has over the making and repeal of delegated legislation. Judicial controls are those exercised by the judges in the courts when people challenge the validity of a particular piece of delegated legislation.

Some enabling Acts require an **affirmative resolution** from Parliament before the delegated legislation can become law. The delegated legislation has to be laid before both Houses, and if a vote to approve it is taken within a specified time, it becomes law. For example, under the **Criminal Justice and Public Order Act 1994** the minister is allowed to make regulations to control sales by ticket touts at sporting events but only if such regulations are specifically approved by Parliament.

Much more delegated legislation is subject to a **negative resolution**. The delegated legislation is put before Parliament, and if no member has put down a motion to annul it within a specified period (usually 40 days) it becomes law.

The **Joint Committee on Statutory Instruments**, with members from both Houses of Parliament (the Scrutiny Committee), reviews all statutory instruments and can draw the attention of Parliament to any that need special consideration. A statutory instrument will be referred back to Parliament if:

- it imposes a tax
- under the Act the statutory instrument cannot be challenged in the courts
- the delegated legislation appears to be retrospectively effective and this was not provided for in the enabling Act
- the powers granted in the Act have been exceeded or used in an unusual way
- the legislation is defective or needs clarification

The Committee has no power to alter the legislation, as it merely reports back on its findings, but it does provide a check on delegated legislation. Parliament itself holds the ultimate safeguard, in that it can withdraw the delegated power and revoke any piece of delegated legislation at any time.

Control by the courts

Unlike a statute, the validity of delegated legislation can be challenged in the courts. Any individual who has a personal interest in the delegated legislation (i.e. who is affected by it) may apply to the courts under the **judicial review** procedure. The grounds for this are that they believe the piece of delegated legislation is *ultra vires*, which means that it goes beyond the powers granted by Parliament. If it is found to be *ultra vires*, the delegated legislation is declared void and ineffective.

This can be in the form of **procedural *ultra vires***, where a public authority has not followed the procedures set out in the enabling Act for creating delegated legislation. In *Agricultural, Horticultural and Forestry Training Board* v *Aylesbury Mushrooms Ltd* (1972), failure by the Minister of Labour to consult interested parties as required by the Act led to the order being declared invalid.

A claim of **substantive *ultra vires*** occurs where the delegated legislation goes beyond the powers granted by the enabling Act. In *R* v *Home Secretary ex parte Fire Brigades Union* (1995), where the home secretary made changes to the Criminal Injuries Compensation Scheme, he was held to have exceeded the power given in the **Criminal Justice Act 1988**. Another example is *R* v *Secretary of State for Health ex parte Pfizer* (1999), in which it was held that a circular from the secretary of state for health advising doctors not to prescribe Viagra went beyond the powers given in the parent Acts.

The courts will also declare invalid any delegated legislation that is unreasonable, under the principle established in *Associated Provincial Picture Houses* v *Wednesbury*

Knowledge check 10

What is procedural *ultra vires*?

Knowledge check 11

What is substantive *ultra vires*?

Corporation (1948). This may be because the rules are unjust, are made in bad faith or are so perverse that no reasonable person would have made them. An example is *Strickland* v *Hayes* (1896), in which a bylaw prohibiting the singing of obscene songs was too widely drawn so that it prohibited the singing of such songs in private as well as in public and was therefore unreasonable.

Effectiveness of the controls on delegated legislation

There are drawbacks to control by Parliament. The use of the affirmative procedure usually draws Parliament's attention to the delegated legislation, but only on rare occasions is it possible to stop the legislation from being passed. The Scrutiny Committee is more important and has managed to have changes made to some pieces of delegated legislation. Its powers are limited, however, as it can only consider whether the delegated powers have been used correctly, and not the merits of the legislation. Its reports are not binding either.

Control by the courts has been successful in many cases, but there are limitations on judicial control. The delegated legislation may have been in force for years before someone affected by it is prepared to challenge it. Another problem is that the discretionary powers conferred on the minister by the enabling Act may be extremely wide, resulting in difficulties in establishing that he or she has acted *ultra vires*.

Advantages of or reasons for delegated legislation

There are a number of reasons why delegated legislation is needed:
- There is not enough time for Parliament to consider every detail of every regulation/ rule. More than 3,000 statutory instruments are passed every year, so delegated legislation allows Parliament to concentrate on broad issues of policy rather than masses of detail. For example, the **Road Traffic Act 1972** provided that motor cyclists had to wear helmets, but the details were left to the minister to publish in the **Motor Cycles (Protective Helmets) Regulations 1980**.
- Parliament does not have the knowledge or technical expertise necessary in certain areas, such as building regulations or health and safety regulations at work. Delegating legislation allows the use of experts in the relevant areas to make the rules as for example in drawing up the **Air Navigation Order 1995** which contains complex technical regulations about civil aviation.
- Local people know local needs. Local authority bylaws, as a result, are more appropriate than broad and general national legislation.
- Delegated legislation can be achieved more quickly than an Act of Parliament. It can also be amended more quickly if circumstances change, allowing flexibility. Orders in Council can be used in emergencies when Parliament is not sitting.
- Delegated legislation is easily revoked if it causes problems. An Act of Parliament would require another statute to amend or revoke it, which would take much longer.

Examiner tip

You can use examples of statutory instruments, bylaws or Orders in Council to illustrate several of these points.

- It is impossible for Parliament to foresee all the problems that might arise when it passes a statute. When problems do arise, delegated legislation to rectify them can be put into place quickly.

Disadvantages of delegated legislation

- The main argument against delegated legislation is that it is undemocratic, because it is made by unelected people rather than by Parliament.
- Much is sub-delegated and made by civil servants in the relevant government departments rather than by the ministers who were originally given the delegated powers. Civil servants are unaccountable to the electorate. (This is not the case with bylaws, as local authorities are elected bodies and accountable to the voters in their area.)
- The large amount of delegated legislation makes it difficult to keep track of the current law. There is little publicity compared to that received by Acts of Parliament, so people may be unaware that a particular piece of legislation exists.
- Control by Parliament is not always effective. Few statutory instruments have affirmative resolution, and MPs are too busy to look at the others. Scrutiny Committee recommendations are often ignored.
- There can be a lack of scrutiny. It has been argued that delegated legislation can be used by governments to make quite significant changes to the law and avoid the inconvenience of submitting them to the scrutiny of the parliamentary process. This is particularly the case with 'Henry VIII clauses', which allow delegated legislation to be used to amend or repeal Acts of Parliament. There was much criticism of the **Legislative and Regulatory Reform Bill** on the basis that it would allow ministers to amend or repeal primary legislation, though the Act when finally passed in 2006 contained significant safeguards and allowed for a super-affirmative procedure for measures introduced under the Act.

Examiner tip

In a question about advantages or disadvantages, try to refer to examples or evidence to support your points.

Summary

Types of delegated legislation:
- Orders in Council
- statutory instruments
- bylaws

Control of delegated legislation:
- parliamentary controls — enabling Act can set limits; affirmative and negative resolution; Delegated Powers Scrutiny Committee and Joint Committee on Statutory Instruments; can repeal enabling clause or revoke any delegated legislation
- judicial controls (by the courts) — anyone can apply for judicial review on the basis that delegated legislation is *ultra vires* (whoever made it has gone beyond their powers):
  - procedural *ultra vires* — the correct procedures have not been followed

  - substantive *ultra vires* — the delegated legislation has gone beyond the powers in the enabling Act
  - unreasonable

Reasons for and advantages of delegated legislation:
- allows Parliament to concentrate on principles rather than detail
- expert or local knowledge
- can be passed quickly and repealed easily

Disadvantages of delegated legislation:
- can be undemocratic, especially if sub-delegation
- lack of scrutiny or effective control by Parliament, especially Henry VIII clauses or if negative procedure used
- little publicity and difficult for public to keep track of it

Statutory interpretation

The process of statutory interpretation is used by judges in the courts when there is a dispute or uncertainty over the meaning of a word or phrase in an Act of Parliament or piece of delegated legislation. The role of the courts is to find out how Parliament intended the law to apply and to carry out this interpretation. It may form a precedent for future cases. The necessity for this can arise for a number of reasons:

- Due to the complexity of the English language, a word may have several meanings, which can lead to ambiguity.
- The meaning of words can change over time.
- The legislation may have been drawn up quickly in response to public concerns and the wording may not be as precise as it should be. A good example is the **Dangerous Dogs Act 1991**, which, drawn up and enacted after a series of incidents during the late summer of 1989 caused great public concern, uses a broad term instead of a limited and specific word.
- The drafting of the original bill may have contained errors. Parliament may not notice errors, especially if there are many amendments during a bill's passage through all the parliamentary stages.
- Changes in technology and social issues can affect how an Act is applied, as in *Royal College of Nursing* v *DHSS* (1981).
- The amount of delegated legislation is increasing.

Aids to statutory interpretation

Judges can use various aids when interpreting a statute. These include internal or intrinsic aids, and external or extrinsic aids.

Internal or intrinsic aids

These are found in the Act itself and may help to make its meaning clear.

- **The long title and the short title of the Act**. In *Cornwall County Council* v *Baker* (2003), the divisional court referred to the long title to confirm the purpose of the **Protection of Animals (Amendment) Act 2000**.
- **The preamble**, if there is one. Older Acts have a detailed preamble outlining what the statute covered and its purpose.
- **Marginal notes and headings**. Some sections of the Act may have headings, and marginal notes are usually added by the person drafting the Act. Both may provide guidance. A marginal note was referred to in *R* v *Tivnan* (1999) in order to clarify whether it was Parliament's intention to deprive drug dealers of assets equivalent in value to the proceeds obtained from drug dealing, and not necessarily just those assets purchased directly from the proceeds of the drug dealing.
- **The interpretation section**. Most Acts now contain interpretation sections. An example is s.10 of the **Theft Act 1968**, which after referring to the use of 'a weapon of offence' in aggravated burglary, defines it as 'any article made or adapted for use for causing injury'.

Examiner tip

Exam questions frequently ask about aids, but you need to look carefully to see whether you are being asked about internal or external aids or both. Also one type of aid may be linked with something else, e.g. rules of language or one of the rules of interpretation. A whole question on one type of aid would obviously require more detail than half a question.

Knowledge check 12

Explain what is meant by intrinsic aids.

Examiner tip

In your exam answer refer to specific parts of Acts as the notes do and try to use examples.

- **Schedules**. Acts often contain schedules, which are found at the end of an Act and include more detailed clarification. An example is Schedule 2 of the **Unfair Contract Terms Act 1977**, which outlines the tests for determining the principle of reasonableness.

Advantages of internal aids

- It is more respectful of Parliament to look elsewhere in the Act than outside the Act.
- It is quick and easy to look at things like marginal notes, which were helpful in *Tivnan*, or at the long title (used in *Cornwall CC v Baker*).
- Some internal aids like interpretation sections and schedules are designed to provide definitions and explanations, so it is common sense to look at them. For example, s.10 of the **Theft Act** explained the meaning of 'weapon of offence'.

Disadvantages of internal aids

- Most problems with wording are not likely to be solved by looking elsewhere in the Act, especially if the words are ambiguous as in *Allen* or very plain but wrong as in *Whitely v Chappell*.
- Internal aids on their own are not likely to be enough, and if judges were not allowed to refer to anything outside the Act it would be more difficult for them to avoid unfair or absurd decisions.

External or extrinsic aids

These are found outside the Act and include the following:

- **Dictionaries** of various kinds. For example, in *Vaughan v Vaughan* (1973), where a man had been pestering his ex-wife, the Court of Appeal used a dictionary in order to define 'molest' and concluded that the definition was wide enough to cover his behaviour. Another example is *Cheeseman* (1990) where a dictionary was used to decide the meaning of the word 'passengers'.
- **Previous Acts of Parliament and earlier case law**. In *Royal Crown Derby Porcelain Co. Ltd v Raymond Russell* (1949), when considering the **Rent and Mortgage Act 1933**, the court interpreted words used in the Act by referring to similar words used in an earlier Act and to the interpretation applied to these words in a number of cases.
- **Reference to *Hansard***, the official report of the proceedings in Parliament. Until 1990, the courts were not allowed to refer to *Hansard* in order to find out Parliament's intention. This was overturned in *Pepper v Hart* (1993). However, this use is restricted to cases where the words of an Act are ambiguous or obscure or lead to an absurdity, and even then, only where there is a clear statement by the minister introducing the legislation that would resolve the doubt. The wider use of *Hansard* is only permitted if the legislation in question has introduced an international convention or European directive into English law. In *Three Rivers DC v Bank of England* (1996), it was held that the *Pepper v Hart* principle did not have to be applied so narrowly because it was important to construe the statute purposively and consistently with any European materials such as directives.
- **Law reform reports** from bodies such as the Law Commission.
- **International treaties**. *Fothergill v Monarch Airlines Ltd* (1980) confirmed that *travaux préparatoires* (background working papers) could be used to ascertain the

Examiner tip

In an exam question you should try to refer to at least three sorts of external aid. Dictionaries are fairly easy to remember. *Hansard* is an important one to mention and try to refer to *Pepper v Hart*.

meaning of an ambiguous or doubtful section of an Act based on an international treaty.

- **Explanatory notes**. Since 1999, all government bills are accompanied by explanatory notes, which provide guidance on complex parts of the bill.

Advantages of external aids

- Using a dictionary is quick and easy as in *Cheeseman* and *Vaughan*.
- Using *Hansard* might clarify what Parliament meant. Lord Denning said that not to use it would be 'like groping around in the dark without putting the light on'.
- Europe allows background papers to be used so it is sensible for English courts to use them when Acts are based on international rules as in *Fothergill* v *Monarch Airlines*.

Knowledge check 13

Explain what is meant by extrinsic aids.

Disadvantages of external aids

- Using *Hansard* may not reveal what Parliament as a whole intended. *Pepper* v *Hart* restricts the courts to considering what ministers said, but Parliament may have decided not to follow the minister's view. Restricting the use to statements by ministers confuses the distinction between executive and legislature.
- Sometimes what the minister said may not be clear. This was the case in *Deegan* and the court therefore ruled that *Hansard* could not be used. In another case Lord Bingham said that if the statement was not clear the courts would be tempted to compare one statement with another and run the risk of questioning proceedings in Parliament, which constitutionally they are not allowed to do.
- There is the danger of treating materials that are not part of the Act as having the same status as the Act and so undermining the authority of Parliament. This is the main objection to using any external aid, though dictionaries are less objectionable than the other external aids and are even used when the literal rule is applied (e.g. *Cheeseman*).

The rules of interpretation

Over the years, judges have developed different approaches to the problem of interpreting statutes. They are usually referred to as 'rules', but more accurately they are 'approaches' because judges are not compelled to follow them as they would be if they were rules. There are traditionally said to be three 'rules' used by judges in interpreting statutes: the literal rule, the golden rule and the mischief rule. There is also now the purposive approach, which is a development of the mischief rule.

Examiner tip

Good answers on any of the rules will refer to case examples. You should make sure that for each of the rules you have cases that you can refer to.

The literal rule

This means giving words their plain, ordinary, dictionary meaning — no matter how unfortunate the consequences. Lord Reid in *Pinner* v *Everett* (1969) referred to 'the natural and ordinary meaning of that word or phrase in its context'.

The rule was used in *Whiteley* v *Chappell* (1868), where the defendant was charged with the offence of impersonating 'any person entitled to vote' at an election. The defendant was acquitted because he impersonated a dead person; applying the literal

Examiner tip

When describing the literal rule try to avoid saying 'in the literal rule you take the words literally'. You need to explain what 'literally' means.

rule, a dead person is not entitled to vote. Another example is *Fisher* v *Bell* (1961), in which a shopkeeper put flick knives on display in his shop window. The **Restriction of Offensive Weapons Act 1959** made it an offence to sell flick knives or offer them for sale. However, the court decided that flick knives on display in a shop window were not an offer to sell but rather an invitation to treat. Therefore, despite the fact that Parliament had legislated to prevent just this sort of display, applying the literal rule meant that the defendant was not guilty, and Parliament had to amend the Act.

This rule has also led to unfair or unjust decisions. In *London and North Eastern Railway Co.* v *Berriman* (1946), Mrs Berriman was unable to obtain compensation when her husband was killed while carrying out maintenance work oiling points on the railway line. The relevant statute said that a lookout should be provided to warn rail workers of approaching trains when relaying or repairing the track; however, Berriman was 'maintaining' the tracks. The words 'relaying' and 'repairing' were given their ordinary meaning.

Despite Lord Denning's observation in *Nothman* v *London Borough of Barnet* (1978) that 'the literal method is now completely out of date', the literal rule is still used by judges. It was used in *Cutter* v *Eagle Star Insurance Co.* (1998), in which the House of Lords decided that the word 'road' in the **Road Traffic Act 1988** could not include a car park, and also in *Cheeseman* (1990), in which the court decided that policemen keeping watch could not be considered to be passengers for the purposes of the **Town Police Causes Act 1847**, with the result that Cheeseman was acquitted of the offence.

Knowledge check 14

What is the literal rule?

Advantages of the literal rule

- It respects the sovereignty of Parliament. Judges who support it argue that if there are mistakes in statutes it is for Parliament not judges to correct them. Lord Simonds in *Magor and St Mellons* v *Newport Corporation* argued that it was not open to judges to fill in gaps in the Act. If a gap was disclosed then 'the remedy lies in an amending Act'. This is what happened following the decision in *Fisher* v *Bell*.
- The rule encourages certainty and people know where they stand. Lord Simon in *Stock* v *Frank Jones* said that it was better to let Parliament make changes rather than having 'judicial contortion' of the law with the result that 'ordinary citizens and their advisers hardly know where they stand'. In other words, it is better to know that what judges are going to do is to take the words literally rather than have the uncertainty of them trying to work out what Parliament may have meant. One result of this might be that people will not waste time and money bringing cases to court.
- Quick decisions can be made. In *Cheeseman*, the word 'passenger' was quickly found in an 1847 dictionary (the year of the statute being interpreted). In *Berriman* it was easy to see that maintaining was not the same as repairing and this would be much quicker than having to work out whether Parliament intended this.

Examiner tip

Notice that you need to develop and explain each advantage and use evidence to back up your point.

Disadvantages of the literal rule

- It can lead to unfair or absurd results. In *LNER* v *Berriman*, the dead railway worker's widow could not claim because he was maintaining not repairing the track. This does not seem fair — his job was just as dangerous as that being done by other railway workers who were protected under the Act. Also it does not seem fair in *Whitely* v *Chappell* that someone would be guilty if they cheated by impersonating a live person but not if they impersonated a dead person. The outcome clearly does not reflect Parliament's intention which was to stop all kinds of electoral fraud and it must have seemed a very silly decision to ordinary people.

- It is hard to apply if words have more than one meaning. In *R* v *Allen*, if 'marry' had been interpreted to have its ordinary meaning, the crime of bigamy could not have been committed. The literal rule does not really allow for a situation where there might be another meaning that is less common but more appropriate.
- It is not flexible and does not allow judges to use common sense. Michael Zander says that it is mechanical and divorced from the realities of the use of language.
- It can result in cases being decided on technicalities. In both *Cheeseman* and the recent case of *Porter* (2006), both men were clearly guilty of the offences, but escaped conviction — in Cheeseman's case because the policemen were not passengers and in Porter's case because the images on his computer could no longer be accessed.

The golden rule

This is a modification of the literal rule and says that judges should use the literal rule unless it would produce an absurd result. There are two views on how far the rule should be used: the narrow application and the wider application.

Under the **narrow application**, proposed by Lord Reid in *Jones* v *DPP* (1962), if a word is ambiguous the judge may choose between possible meanings of the word in order to avoid an absurd outcome. He argued that if a word had more than one meaning, 'then you can choose between those meanings, but beyond this you cannot go'.

This application was used in *R* v *Allen* (1872). Section 57 of the **Offences Against the Person Act 1861** made it an offence to marry if you were already married to someone else. The court decided that 'marry' was ambiguous and could have two meanings: to become legally married or to go through a ceremony of marriage. Allen sought to rely on the first definition and argued that since he was already married, his second marriage could not be valid, so he could not be guilty of bigamy. However, it was clearly absurd to apply the first meaning, as no one could then be convicted of the offence. Therefore, the judge chose the second meaning and Allen was found guilty.

The **wider application** is where there is only one meaning but this would lead to an absurd or repugnant situation. In *Adler* v *George* (1964), s.3 of **the Official Secrets Act 1920** made it an offence to be found 'in the vicinity of a prohibited place'. The accused was arrested *inside* the prohibited place; therefore, he argued that he could not be convicted. Lord Parker CJ used the golden rule and held that 'in the vicinity of' could mean 'being in or in the vicinity of' the prohibited place. Another example is *Re Sigsworth* (1935), in which the court prevented a son who had murdered his mother from inheriting his mother's estate under the intestacy rules set out in the **Administration of Estates Act 1925**. The wording of the Act was unambiguous, but the court did not want the murderer to benefit from his crime.

Examiner tip

The good points about the literal rule are similar to the bad points about the mischief and purposive rules and vice versa. Rigidly following the wording in an Act can produce undesirable results, but it prevents judges doing what should be Parliament's job. Interpreting words in the light of the mischief or purpose allows judges to achieve sensible outcomes, but it is not their job to rewrite statutes.

Examiner tip

The golden rule is rather complicated because there are two views on how it should be used. For high marks you should try to refer to both applications. But it is also important to stress that the golden rule involves using the literal rule in most circumstances. It is only in extreme cases, where using the literal rule would produce a ridiculous or objectionable result, that judges should consider changing the words in an Act.

Advantages of the golden rule

- Courts can alter the wording of a statute if the result is absurd or repugnant. This is clearly sensible. In *R* v *Allen* the court altered the meaning of the word 'marry' because otherwise the outcome would have been absurd. The golden rule was also used in *Sigsworth* because it would clearly have been repugnant that he should have been able to benefit from his crime.
- It prevents Parliament from having to pass amending legislation. The court can often make a correction easily by altering just a couple of words, e.g. saying 'on or in the vicinity of' in *Adler* v *George*.
- It respects the authority of Parliament because the literal rule will usually be used. In *Berriman*'s case, the literal rule would still be applied because the words used only have one meaning, so it respects Parliament's authority in the majority of cases. Under the narrow application you can only choose between alternative meanings of words, so this is clearly respecting the authority of Parliament. The wider application will actually change the wording, but it will only be applied in extreme situations as in *Sigsworth*.

Knowledge check 15

What are the two applications of the golden rule?

Disadvantages of the golden rule

- It only allows judges to change the wording of statutes in very limited circumstances. Michael Zander (an academic and critic of this rule) describes it as 'a feeble parachute' because it is not of much use. It could not be used in cases like *Berriman* because although the situation could be considered unfair it was not absurd or repugnant.
- It is unpredictable and lacks guidelines. Michael Zander describes it as 'an unpredictable safety valve' due to the lack of guidelines as to when it should be used. The Law Commission (1969) argued that the rule was of limited value and noted that the rule provided no clear means to test what the idea of absurdity meant. It is made more unpredictable by the fact that there are two approaches and some judges like Lord Reid clearly felt that you could not go further than the narrow approach while others have used the wider approach in cases like *Sigsworth* and *Adler* v *George*.
- Its application is inconsistent. This can even be true when the same judge is involved. Lord Parker CJ used the golden rule in *Adler* v *George* but the literal rule in *Fisher* v *Bell* where the outcome seemed just as absurd.

The mischief rule

This rule was laid down in *Heydon*'s case (1584). Judges should consider four factors when using this rule:

(1) What was the common law before the Act was passed?
(2) What was the mischief that the Act was designed to remedy?
(3) What was the remedy that Parliament was trying to provide?
(4) What was the reason for the remedy?

Judges should look for the 'mischief' the Act was designed to remedy and interpret the Act in such a way that a remedy is achieved. This may mean disregarding the other rules.

This rule was used in *Smith* v *Hughes* (1960), where 'soliciting in the street' in the **Street Offences Act 1959** was held to include soliciting from the window of a house. The court said that the aim of the Act was to allow people to walk along the streets without being solicited, and it should be interpreted to cover this situation. In *Royal College of Nursing* v *DHSS* (1981), the court had to consider the wording of the Abortion Act 1967, which stated that pregnancies had to be terminated by a 'registered medical practitioner'. The House of Lords looked at the mischief that Parliament was aiming to redress — illegal, 'backstreet' abortions — and decided that having nurses (rather than doctors) supervising part of the abortion procedure was not unlawful.

There are limitations on the use of the mischief rule. In *Jones* v *Wrotham Park* (1980), Lord Diplock said that it could only be used where:

- the mischief could be seen clearly from the Act
- it was apparent that Parliament had overlooked the problem
- additional words required could be stated with a high degree of certainty

Advantages of the mischief rule

- It gives effect to Parliament's intentions. In *Smith* v *Hughes*, it was clearly Parliament's intention to stop prostitutes from being a nuisance to others, whether they were literally in the street or not. Equally, in *Elliott* v *Grey*, Parliament would have wanted all vehicles on the road to be insured.
- It allows judges to use their common sense and saves Parliament from having to pass an amending Act. Lord Denning said in *Magor and St Mellons* v *Newport Corporation* that it allowed judges to 'fill in the gaps' when Parliament had left something out. In *Nothman* v *London Borough of Barnet* he said that judges should use their good sense to do what Parliament would have done if it had had the situation in mind.
- It allows judges to consider social and technological changes. The decision of the House of Lords in *RCN* v *DHSS* recognised that medical practice had changed since the passing of the Abortion Act.
- It allows judges to look at external aids like *Hansard* as in *Pepper* v *Hart* or international treaties as in *Fothergill* v *Monarch Airlines*. If the use of these helps judges to see what Parliament intended then it is sensible to use them.

Disadvantages of the mischief rule

- Finding the intention of Parliament can be difficult. Referring to what a minister has said in Parliament as *Pepper* v *Hart* allows may not reflect what Parliament as a whole intended. It is reasonable to argue that what Parliament intended can only be seen in what it actually wrote in an Act and that *Smith* v *Hughes* is wrongly decided because if Parliament had intended the **Street Offences Act** to apply to prostitutes in houses it would have said so.
- It is undemocratic. It gives too much power to unelected judges. In the *Magor and St Mellons* case Lord Simonds described its use as 'a naked usurpation of the legislative function under the thin disguise of interpretation'. He added that judges were to be guided by Parliament's enactments and not by its intentions. The democratic solution would be for Parliament to pass an amending Act.

Examiner tip

The mischief and the purposive rules are very similar in that they are based on trying to find out what Parliament really intended. The mischief rule is obviously much older and quite narrow in that it focuses on the mischief or the evil that the Act was designed to put right. The purposive rule is much simpler as it requires judges to look at what Parliament was aiming to achieve through the Act and to interpret any difficult words in the light of this purpose.

Knowledge check 16

How does the mischief rule work?

- The rule is out of date and does not reflect modern needs. The role of judges has changed. They no longer draft statutes for the monarch as they did in the sixteenth century when *Heydon*'s case was passed.
- It might cause confusion if a judge changes the meaning of a statute. In *Stock* v *Frank Jones,* Lord Simon refused to alter the words of a statute because it would have the result that 'ordinary citizens and their advisers hardly know where they stand'.

The purposive approach

This approach requires the court to examine the object of the Act and to construe doubtful passages in accordance with that purpose.

Over the last 20 years, the purposive approach has gained ground. The European Court of Justice uses this approach in interpreting EU law, and the English courts have to use the same approach when interpreting domestic legislation brought in as a result of this. The **Human Rights Act 1998** is also likely to cause a shift towards the purposive approach.

A good example of its use is *Jones* v *Tower Boot Co.* (1997), in which the Court of Appeal decided that racial harassment by fellow workers happened 'in the course of employment', making the employer liable. The Court of Appeal said that it was right to give the words a meaning other than their natural meaning so that the purpose of the legislation could be achieved.

Another example is *Coltman* v *Bibby Tankers* (1987), in which the House of Lords had to decide whether a ship, which had sunk, could be considered to be 'equipment' for the purposes of the **Employers' Liability (Defective Equipment) Act 1969**. Equipment was defined in the Act as including 'any plant and machinery, vehicle, aircraft and clothing', but the Law Lords decided that the purpose of the Act was clearly to protect workers in the workplace, and that as the ship had been defective in design and had caused death when it sank, it would be right to give the provision a broad construction.

The approach was also used in *R* v *Registrar General ex parte Smith* (1990) in which the court decided that although the **Adoption Act 1976** allowed people who had been adopted to find out the identity of their natural parents, it was clearly not Parliament's purpose to allow people to get this information if they were likely to pose a threat to the parent. Smith had already committed two murders and was mentally ill and posed a risk to his mother, so the court felt that Parliament would have wanted his mother to be protected.

Advantages of the purposive approach

- It makes sense to look at the whole purpose of the Act. In the twenty-first century judges should be able to look at what the Act was designed to do rather than just look for the mischief. The purposive approach is widely used in most other EU countries and is therefore more relevant than the rules set out in *Heydon*'s case which dates from Tudor times.
- It gives effect to Parliament's intentions. Supporters of the rule would argue that Parliament clearly intended in **Employers' Liability (Defective Equipment) Act 1969** to protect workers in the workplace and therefore it was reasonable in *Coltman* v *Bibby Tankers* to include ships as equipment even though Parliament had not specifically done so.

- It allows judges to use their common sense. Lord Denning said in *Magor and St Mellons* v *Newport Corporation* that it allowed judges to 'fill in the gaps' when Parliament had left something out. In *Nothman* v *London Borough of Barnet* he said that judges should use their good sense to do what Parliament would have done if it had had the situation in mind. It is also sensible to use external aids like *Hansard* as in *Pepper* v *Hart* or international treaties as in *Fothergill* v *Monarch Airlines* if the use of these helps judges to see what Parliament intended.
- It allows judges to consider social and technological changes. The decision of the House of Lords in *RCN* v *DHSS* recognised that medical practice had changed since the passing of the **Abortion Act**.

Disadvantages of the purposive approach

- Finding the intention of Parliament can be difficult. Referring to what a minister has said in Parliament as *Pepper* v *Hart* allows may not reflect what Parliament as a whole intended. In *R* v *Deegan,* an application to consider *Hansard* was rejected because what ministers had said was not sufficiently clear. It is reasonable to argue that what Parliament intended can only be seen in what it actually wrote in an Act and *Coltman* v *Bibby Tankers* is wrongly decided because if Parliament had intended the Act to apply to ships it would have said so.
- It is undemocratic. It gives too much power to unelected judges. In the *Magor and St Mellons* case Lord Simonds described its use as 'a naked usurpation of the legislative function under the thin disguise of interpretation'. He added that judges were to be guided by Parliament's enactments and not by their intentions. The democratic solution would be for Parliament to pass an amending Act.
- It might cause confusion if a judge changes the meaning of a statute. In *Stock* v *Frank Jones,* Lord Simon refused to alter the words of a statute because it would have the result that 'ordinary citizens and their advisers hardly know where they stand'.

> **Examiner tip**
>
> The advantages and disadvantages of the mischief and purposive rules apply to both. Even some of the cases can be used to illustrate either rule. If when discussing advantages or disadvantages you are asked to chose two rules it would be better not to choose the mischief and the purposive because they are so similar.

Rules of language

These are common-sense rules that have been developed over time. They allow the judges to look at other words in the Act in order to make the meaning of words and phrases clear. The rules are:

- *ejusdem generis*: in a list, general words that follow specific words are limited to the same type as the specific ones. If an Act uses the phrase 'dogs, cats and other animals', the 'other animals' would include other domestic animals but not wild animals. In *Re Stockport Ragged, Industrial and Reformatory Schools* (1898), the courts had to consider the phrase 'cathedral, collegiate, chapter and other schools'. They decided that 'other schools' had to be limited to schools of the same kind as those in the list, which were all Church schools. The rule was also applied in *Powell* v *Kempton Park Racecourse* (1899), in which the court concluded that 'house, office, room or other place for betting' could not include open-air betting on the racecourse itself, because places specified in the list were all indoors.
- *expressio unius est exclusio alterius*: express mention of one thing implies the exclusion of another. If an Act specifically referred to Labrador dogs, it would not include other breeds of dog. An example is *Tempest* v *Kilner* (1846), where a section of an Act included the words 'goods, wares and merchandise'. It was held that the

Knowledge check 18

Name two rules of language.

Examiner tip

Make sure you read the exam question carefully and note whether you are asked to write about rules of language or one of the rules of interpretation, which are sometimes called rules of construction.

section could not be taken to apply to stocks and shares, as they had not been included in the list. In *R v Inhabitants of Sedgeley* (1831) an Act referred in a list to coal mines. It could not apply to other types of mine.

- ***noscitur a sociis***: a word draws meaning from other words around it. For example, in *Inland Revenue Commissioners* v *Frere* (1965), a section of an Act referred to 'interest, annuities or other annual interest'. Because of the reference 'other annual interest', the court decided that the first use of 'interest' must be restricted to annual interest (and therefore not apply to daily or monthly interest).

Conclusion

The courts are not told how to solve a particular problem. There is no indication, either in the 'rules' or elsewhere, as to which approach should be taken in any given situation. In recent years, the courts have moved towards using the purposive approach and new extrinsic aids. However, the individual judge selects the method that he or she wishes to use when interpreting a statute. This could result in one judge using the literal approach, while another uses the purposive approach, with the two reaching opposite conclusions.

Summary

Aids to statutory interpretation. Judges sometimes have to try to interpret or make sense of difficult or ambiguous words in statutes. They have various tools available to help them:

- internal aids — they can look elsewhere in the Act for guidance
- external aids — they can look at various other documents like dictionaries

Rules of interpretation. Judges can choose to use one of four rules of interpretation:

- Literal rule. Judges follow the wording as it is written and give words their plain ordinary meaning. The main advantages are that it respects the authority of Parliament and encourages certainty so that people know where they stand. The main disadvantages are that it may lead to absurd or unfair decisions and does not allow judges to use their common sense.
- Golden rule. Judges use the literal rule unless the result would be absurd. Under the narrow application they can only use it when the difficulty is caused by a word having more than one meaning. The wider application allows words to be altered in situations where there would otherwise be an absurd or repugnant outcome. The main advantage is that it allows judges to avoid absurd or repugnant decisions and the disadvantage is that it can only be used in very limited circumstances.

- Mischief rule. Judges try to find out what Parliament intended by looking at the problem the Act was designed to put right. Advantages of the mischief rule include the fact that it allows judges to use their common sense and try to carry out Parliament's real intention. This saves Parliament having to pass an amending Act. But the disadvantages are that it is undemocratic and that it may be difficult to work out what the problem was that the Act was designed to overcome.
- Purposive rule. This is a more modern version of the mischief rule and requires judges to look for the purpose behind the Act and interpret words in accordance with that purpose. The main advantages of the purposive rule are the same as for the mischief rule, with the additional benefits that it is more up to date and fits in better with what is done in Europe. The disadvantages are the same as for the mischief rule.

Rules of language. These are common-sense rules that apply when particular combinations of words are used:

- *ejusdem generis*
- *expressio unius*
- *noscitur a sociis*

Judicial precedent

When the facts of a case are similar to a case that has already been decided, the judge must follow that previous decision, especially if it was reached by a higher court. This forms the basis of judicial precedent and is known as **stare decisis**, 'stand by the decision'.

The hierarchy of the courts

In order for the system of judicial precedent to work, there must be rules for judges to follow to make sure there is consistency in the law. One way of doing this is to have a hierarchy, so that decisions in the higher courts bind the lower courts. Some of the courts are also bound by their own previous decisions.

The European Court of Justice

Since the UK joined the European Community in 1973, decisions made by the European Court of Justice (ECJ) have been binding on all the courts in the UK in matters of EU law (e.g. the interpretation of treaties). The ECJ is not bound by its own previous decisions and can overrule them.

The Supreme Court

The Supreme Court replaced the House of Lords in October 2009 as the most senior English Court. It is bound by the decisions of the ECJ, but as the highest appeal court in England, its decisions bind all the other English courts. Originally, except where a decision was made **per incuriam** ('in error'), the House of Lords was bound by its own previous decisions. This was established in *London Street Tramways* v *London County Council* (1898), in order to ensure certainty in the law. However, in 1966 the Lord Chancellor issued a **Practice Statement**, which allowed the House of Lords to depart from an earlier decision 'when it appears right to do so'.

The House of Lords has used the power sparingly. Examples include:
- *British Railways Board* v *Herrington* (1972) overruled *Addie* v *Dumbreck* (1929) on the duty of care owed to a child trespasser.
- *Pepper* v *Hart* (1993) overruled the House of Lords ruling in *Davis* v *Johnson* (1979) that banned the use of *Hansard* in statutory interpretation.
- *R* v *Shivpuri* (1986) overruled *Anderton* v *Ryan* (1985) on attempting the impossible in theft.
- *R* v *Howe* (1987) overruled *R* v *Lynch* (1975) and stated that duress was no defence to a murder charge.

The Practice Rules of the Supreme Court allow for it to operate a similar system to that under the Practice Statement.

The Court of Appeal

This court has two divisions, which deal solely with either civil cases or criminal cases. Both divisions are bound by decisions of the Supreme Court and the ECJ, but the decisions of one division do not bind the other.

The Court of Appeal (Civil Division)

This division of the Court of Appeal is bound by its own previous decisions. The case of *Young* v *Bristol Aeroplane Co. Ltd* (1944) confirmed this, but set out three exceptions when the Civil Division can depart from its own previous decisions:

- The previous decision was made *per incuriam*, for example the decision was made without considering a relevant Act of Parliament.
- There are two Court of Appeal decisions that conflict.
- A later decision of the House of Lords overrules a previous decision in the Court of Appeal.

In the past, the Court of Appeal tried to argue that the Practice Statement should also apply to it, but in *Davis* v *Johnson* (1979) the House of Lords reaffirmed the rule in *Young*.

Note, however, that there are now two additional exceptions to the rule:

- It seems clear following s.3 of the **European Communities Act 1972** that the Court of Appeal can ignore a previous decision that is inconsistent with European Community law or a decision of the ECJ.
- Similarly, in s.2 of the **Human Rights Act 1998** the courts are bound to take into account judgements of the European Court of Human Rights, and presumably apply them rather than a previous Court of Appeal judgement.

The Court of Appeal (Criminal Division)

This division is usually bound by its own previous decisions but may take a more flexible approach if the liberty of an individual is involved. This was upheld in *R* v *Spencer* (1985). In *R* v *Simpson* (2003), a five-person Court of Appeal decided that it would overrule an earlier decision, not because the liberty of the defendant was at issue, but rather to ensure justice for the public at large and maintain confidence in the criminal justice system. The exceptions in *Young* also apply.

Knowledge check 21

What principle did *Young* v *Bristol Aeroplane Co. Ltd* confirm?

The High Court

The divisional courts and the ordinary High Court are all bound by the decisions of the Court of Appeal, the House of Lords and the ECJ. The Family Division and the Chancery Division (civil courts) are bound by their own previous decisions. There is more flexibility in the Queen's Bench Division when hearing appeals on criminal cases. The ordinary High Court is bound by the decisions of the divisional courts but not by its own previous decisions.

The Crown Court

This court is bound by the decisions of all the higher courts. Its decisions are not binding precedent, although the decisions of High Court judges sitting in the Crown Court could form persuasive precedent if reported. The court is not bound to follow its own decisions.

Magistrates' and County Courts

These courts are bound by the courts above them, but their own decisions do not form binding or persuasive precedent. They are not bound by their own previous decisions.

Ratio decidendi and binding precedent

When a judge, after hearing a case, presents his or her written judgement, this is known as **case law**. This judgement sets out the facts of the case and the legal principles that he or she has used to reach a decision. The legal principles are known as the ***ratio decidendi***, 'the reason for deciding'. This is the binding precedent for future cases where the facts are sufficiently similar and where the original case is decided in a court more senior (or, in some cases, at the same level) in the hierarchy. An example of *ratio decidendi* is the rule in *R* v *Nedrick* (1986), confirmed in *R* v *Woollin* (1997), that if a jury considers that the defendant foresaw death or serious injury as a virtual certainty, oblique intention may be inferred. Another example is the judgement in *R* v *Cunningham* (1957) that to be reckless you have to know there is a risk of an unlawful consequence and decide to take the risk.

Knowledge check 22

Explain what is meant by *ratio decidendi*.

Persuasive precedent

Persuasive precedent is precedent that judges in future cases may choose to follow, but they are not bound to.

Obiter dicta statements

Sometimes the judge may speculate on what the decision might have been if the situation were different. This is known as ***obiter dicta***, 'things said by the way'. Although this is not part of the case law, it may influence judges in later cases as persuasive precedent. Lord Denning's *obiter dicta* statements in the case of *Central London Property Trust Ltd* v *High Trees House Ltd* (1947) led to the creation of the doctrine of **promissory estoppel**.

The *obiter dicta* statement in *R* v *Howe* (1987) that duress was not available to a charge of attempted murder was followed in *R* v *Gotts* (1992).

Another good example is in *Hall* v *Simons* (2000), which concerned allegedly negligent advice given by solicitors. Lord Hoffman's statement, that the rule giving advocates immunity for alleged negligence was no longer appropriate and should be abolished, is technically *obiter dicta*, but it has been treated as authoritative and will almost certainly be followed in future cases.

Knowledge check 23

Explain what is meant by *obiter dicta*.

Examiner tip

A question may ask you to say what *obiter dicta* means or it may ask you to explain what is meant by persuasive precedent. This includes *obiter dicta*, but it would also require you to consider other types of persuasive precedent.

Courts lower in the hierarchy

Persuasive precedent may also arise from the lower courts. The House of Lords agreed with the reasons that the Court of Appeal gave in the case of *R* v *R* (1991) when deciding that a man could be found guilty of raping his wife.

Dissenting judgements

When a court reaches a majority decision (in the Court of Appeal a case is usually heard by three judges, in the House of Lords by five), the dissenting judge(s) have to give their reasons for dissenting. If the case goes to appeal in a higher court, these reasons may be followed as persuasive precedent if the higher court disagrees with the majority decision of the lower court. For example, the dissenting judgement of Lord Denning in *Candler* v *Crane Christmas* (1951) was followed by the House of Lords in *Heller* v *Hedley Byrne* (1964).

Decisions of the Judicial Committee of the Privy Council

Decisions of the Judicial Committee of the Privy Council (JCPC) are made as a result of its role as a court of final appeal for some Commonwealth countries (many of the judges in the court are members of the House of Lords and therefore very senior judges). These decisions are not binding on the English courts but they can also form persuasive precedent. The Court of Appeal in *Doughty* v *Turner Manufacturing Co. Ltd* (1964) chose to follow the JCPC decision, involving liability and remoteness of damage in the tort of negligence, in *The Wagon Mound No 1* (1961), rather than its own earlier decision in *Re Polemis* (1921).

The Privy Council decision in *Attorney General for Jersey* v *Holley* (2005) concerning the defence of provocation was followed by the Court of Appeal in *R* v *James*, *R* v *Karami* (2006) rather than the House of Lords ruling in *R* v *Smith* (2000).

Decisions in other countries

Sometimes the decisions of courts in the other Commonwealth countries, such as Canada, Australia and New Zealand, become persuasive precedent. For instance, in *Caparo* v *Dickman* (1990), the House of Lords approved a statement in an Australian case.

Law reporting

For the doctrine of judicial precedent to work properly there must be some way in which judges can find out if there are binding precedents in existence. This is achieved by an accurate record of law reporting. It is only since the development of modern law reporting in 1865 that systematic reporting has allowed the proper development of the system of precedent. Even today, there is no 'official set' of law reports, nor is there any official selection of the cases to be reported. The most authoritative set of reports are those produced by the Incorporated Council of Law Reporting (ICLR), set up for this purpose by the Law Society and the Inns of Court in 1865. They are known simply as 'The Law Reports' or as the 'Appeal Cases' (AC), and they report cases from the House of Lords, the Court of Appeal and the divisional courts of the High Court. A separate volume of *Weekly Law Reports* is also published by the ICLR. The *All England Law Reports* published by Butterworths appear weekly and may report cases

Knowledge check 24

What is meant by persuasive precedent?

which do not appear in the ICLR Law Reports. There are also specialised reports, such as the Family Law Reports and the Criminal Appeal Reports.

Many recent cases are now reported on the internet or on CD-ROMs and are often available within hours of the judgements being handed down. There are subscription services such as LexisNexis (the oldest of its kind) and Justis, and many case reports are available free.

How judges avoid following precedent

There are several approaches which judges can take in order to avoid following precedent.

Distinguishing

If the judge finds that the facts of a case are sufficiently different from the case setting the precedent, he or she can distinguish the two cases and avoid following precedent. In *King* v *Phillips* (1953), the Court of Appeal said that a mother who suffered shock after seeing her child's tricycle under a taxi and hearing the child scream was not owed a duty of care as the child was not injured in any way. In *Boardman* v *Sanderson* (1964), however, the claimaint's son was injured when the defendant negligently backed his car over him. The claimant was close by, heard the screams and suffered from shock; he was able to recover damages. The claim failed in the first case as the child was not injured, but in the second case the facts were distinguished because the child was injured and the case succeeded. Another example is *R* v *Wilson*, which was distinguished from *R* v *Brown and others*. In *Brown* the defence of consent was not allowed as sadomasochistic acts did not qualify as surgery or tattooing, but in *Wilson*, where a man carved his initials into his wife's buttocks with a hot knife, the court distinguished *Brown* and said that this did amount to tattooing.

In *Balfour* v *Balfour* (1919), Mrs Balfour was unable to enforce a maintenance agreement made with her husband. The *ratio decidendi* of the case was that there is no intention to create legal relations when agreements are made within marriage. In *Merritt* v *Merritt* (1970), however, the defendant husband sought to rely on the *Balfour* principle to avoid honouring an agreement he had made with his estranged wife. The court distinguished the case on the material difference that the agreement, albeit made within marriage, had been made after the couple had separated, and the husband had to transfer the house to the wife as agreed. The decision limited the scope of the *Balfour* principle and created a new rule in respect of separated couples.

Overruling

Judges in the higher courts can overrule the decisions of the lower courts if they consider the legal principles to be wrong. As stated previously, the 1966 Practice Statement allowed the House of Lords to depart from its own previous decisions, although it has rarely done so. An example is *Pepper* v *Hart* (1993), which overruled *Davis* v *Johnson* (1979) on the issue of whether *Hansard* could be referred to by judges interpreting statutes. The Supreme Court also has this power.

> **Knowledge check 25**
>
> Why is law reporting important?

> **Examiner tip**
>
> A question asking you the main features of precedent would require you to briefly describe hierarchy, *ratio* and law reports.

> **Knowledge check 26**
>
> What is meant by distinguishing?

The Court of Appeal Civil Division has the power to overrule its own earlier decisions, but only in the limited circumstances set out in *Young* v *Bristol Aeroplane Co. Ltd* (1944). The Criminal Division has rather more freedom. In *R* v *Simpson* (2003), it was able to overrule an earlier decision on the basis that justice needed to be achieved for the public at large and that confidence needed to be maintained in the criminal justice system.

Disapproving

Sometimes a judge may be unable to change a decision (e.g. because the precedent is from a higher court), but feels that the decision is wrong. Judges can state that they disapprove the earlier decision and the disapproval may influence decisions in later cases.

Advantages of precedent

Certainty and consistency

Certainty allows people to know what the law is, enabling lawyers to predict the likely outcome of a case. Without a system of binding precedent people could not be sure that the law would stay the same and that would make planning for the future much more difficult. Sir Rupert Cross described precedent as 'a strong cement'. Commenting in *Knuller* v *DPP*, Lord Reid said 'in the interests of certainty', there had to be a good reason for changing a precedent. Consistency is important because people need to be sure that cases that are similar will be dealt with in a similar way.

Flexibility

Flexibility arises through the use of overruling, distinguishing and reversing, allowing the law to evolve. Changes in attitude in society can be taken into account, an example being *R* v *R* (1991), when the House of Lords accepted that a man could be guilty of raping his wife.

Another example is *R* v *Malcherek and Steel* (1981), when the law was adapted to deal with the effect of life-support systems on judging what constitutes the exact point of death. The decision in *Malcherek* was that if the patient is already pronounced brain dead, switching off the life-support machine does not break the chain of causation between the initial injury and the death.

Based on real-life situations

Because the law is made from actual cases it becomes very precise and builds up to a large body of law covering almost every situation. It is also likely that the law will have developed in a common-sense way. This is better than having Parliament legislate in a theoretical way.

Disadvantages of precedent

Complexity and volume

The number of reported cases is large and growing continually. This makes it difficult to know all the cases that might be relevant. Judges may only be aware of those precedents that the parties concerned bring to their attention. There is also difficulty in determining the *ratio decidendi* of some reported cases because of the way in which the judgement is written.

Rigidity

The strict hierarchy means that judges have to follow binding precedent. Therefore, bad or inappropriate decisions cannot be changed unless they are heard in a higher court that can overrule them.

Unsystematic development

Judges can only make law on the facts of the case before them. They cannot lay down a comprehensive code to cover all possible situations, as Parliament can. It is sometimes not helpful when small changes are made, when what is really needed is reform of the whole area of law. For example, in 1994 judges in *Adomako* reintroduced gross negligence manslaughter, when really the whole law on involuntary manslaughter needed systematic reform.

Illogical distinctions

The use of distinguishing, in order to avoid precedent, has led to complexity in some areas of law. There may be only minute and apparently illogical differences between some cases. Too many distinctions of this type can lead to unpredictability.

Lack of democracy

When deciding cases in this way, judges are actually making law, which under the doctrine of the separation of powers is not part of their role.

Lack of research

In order to decide a case, a judge is only presented with the facts of the case and any legal arguments. Unlike Parliament, judges cannot commission research to assess the implications of their decisions.

Retrospective effect

Unlike legislation, which only applies to events after it has come into effect, case law applies retrospectively to events that occurred before the case was brought. This could lead to unfairness if as a result of the case the law is changed, because the parties to the case could not have known what the law was prior to their actions. This is what happened in *R* v *R* (1991), for example, the effect of which was to turn an act that was lawful at the time it was committed into a serious criminal offence.

> **Examiner tip**
> If you are asked to discuss advantages or disadvantages you need to explain why the particular point is an advantage or disadvantage. Your answer should also refer to examples or evidence.

Hierarchy of the courts: the basis of precedent is that judges must follow decisions made by the higher courts:

- Lower courts have to follow decisions made in higher courts.
- The Supreme Court is able to overrule lower court decisions or its own earlier decisions (or House of Lords' decisions) using the Practice Statement.
- The Court of Appeal can overrule lower court decisions, but the Civil Division has limited power to overrule its own earlier decisions (*Young* v *Bristol Aeroplane Co. Ltd*). The Criminal Division has more flexibility.

Ratio decidendi and binding precedent: the part of the judgement that gives the reasons for the decision is known as the *ratio decidendi* and becomes a binding precedent for future cases.

Persuasive precedent: this does not have to be followed, but may influence judges in later cases. It can arise in a number of ways:

- *obiter dicta* — parts of a judgement that are not part of the reasons for the decision

- courts lower in the hierarchy
- dissenting judgements
- decisions of the Judicial Committee of the Privy Council
- decisions in other countries

How judges avoid following precedent:

- distinguishing
- overruling
- disapproving

Advantages of precedent:

- certainty and consistency
- flexibility
- based on real-life situations

Disadvantages of precedent:

- complexity and volume
- the law has developed in an unsystematic way and is unstructured
- case law operates retrospectively

Section B: The legal system

The courts system

It is important that you understand the jurisdiction of the different courts in England and Wales — both civil and criminal — and the process of appeals to the Court of Appeal and the Supreme Court.

Civil courts

Civil disputes involve individuals bringing claims against other individuals. Such claims can arise within the areas of contract, tort, land, employment and family law.

County Courts

There are more than 300 County Courts in England and Wales, which handle the majority of civil cases. They are situated in all large towns and cities, and their procedures are governed by the **County Courts Act 1984**. Trials are usually presided over by a circuit judge, although Recorders and district judges also sit in cases.

The jurisdiction of the County Court

The County Court has jurisdiction over a specific locality, within which defendants must live. If the defendant is a company, the registered office must be situated there.

All contract claims and almost all tort actions up to a value of £50,000 can be tried in the County Courts. Most County Courts can deal with undefended divorce actions. Unless the legal issue in a family law case is particularly complicated, most of these cases are also dealt with by this court, especially probate (finalising the value of a deceased person's estate). The County Court can also hear bankruptcy cases, tax cases and land law disputes, most often those involving repossession orders sought by banks and building societies against home owners in arrears with mortgage payments.

Note that under the Civil Procedure Rules (CPR), which implemented the Woolf Access to Justice recommendations, all fast-track actions must be taken in the County Court. Appeals are heard by a circuit judge (small claims cases), a single High Court judge (fast-track cases) or a Court of Appeal (multi-track cases). In all cases, leave to appeal must be granted.

Knowledge check 28

What is the jurisdiction of the County Court?

The High Court

This court has three divisions:
- **Queen's Bench Division.** This is the main court. It deals with contract and tort cases like negligence. Most cases will involve claims for more than £50,000, but it is possible to bring complex cases over £25,000 here rather than in the County Court. About 70 judges sit in this division.

Knowledge check 29

What is the jurisdiction of each of the three divisions of the High Court?

- **Family Division.** This hears all kinds of family cases including divorce, adoption and care proceedings. There are 18 Family High Court judges.
- **Chancery Division.** This deals with cases such as partnership or company disputes and disputes over wills or trusts or the sale of land. There are 18 Chancery judges.

Appeals from the High Court

These usually go to the **Court of Appeal (Civil Division)**. However, in cases where there is a point of law of general importance it is possible under the **Administration of Justice Act 1969** to leapfrog the Court of Appeal and go straight to the Supreme Court.

From the Court of Appeal a further appeal can be made to the **Supreme Court** set up under the **Constitutional Reform Act 2005**, which replaced the House of Lords in October 2009. But this is only possible if there is a point of law of general public importance and in practice there are likely to be fewer than 100 such cases each year. There are 12 judges in the Supreme Court, though probably only 5 will hear each case, as happened in the House of Lords.

Case management

This is the most significant innovation of the 1999 reforms: the court is the active manager of the litigation. Traditionally, the parties and their lawyers were left to manage their cases. However, the new rules aim to bring cases to trial quickly and efficiently, placing the management of cases in the hands of the judges and emphasising the court's duty to take a proactive role in the administration of each case.

Once proceedings have commenced, the court's powers of case management are triggered by the filing of a defence and/or counterclaim. The court first needs to allocate the case to one of three tracks, which determines the future conduct of the proceedings:

- **small claims** — actions under £5,000 (up to £1,000 for personal injury cases)
- **fast-track** — actions between £5,000 and £25,000
- **multi-track** — actions over £25,000

Small claims arbitration procedure

Within the County Court is the small claims arbitration procedure, which currently has a jurisdiction to hear cases up to a value of £5,000 (£1000 in personal injury cases). A district judge presides over this less formal procedure, where parties are usually unrepresented (as legal aid is not available) and costs are not awarded to the successful party. Most actions heard are for debt recovery and consumer problems. This arbitration has dealt with many cases that could not have been pursued in the County Court itself because of the high costs, delay and complexity. However, there have been problems over enforcement of court orders: about one third of successful claimants have been unable to recover their award of damages.

Fast-track

These cases are normally dealt with in the County Court. The court gives directions for the management of the case and sets a timetable for the disclosure, the exchange of witness statements, the exchange of expert witnesses and the trial date, or the period within which the trial will take place, which will be no more than 30 weeks later.

Multi-track

Generally, cases involving claims for less than £50,000 would be tried in the County Court by a circuit judge, and cases over that limit would be heard in the High Court.

The court can give directions for the management of a multi-track case and can set a timetable for the steps to be taken. Alternatively, for more serious cases, the court may fix a case management conference or a pre-trial review or both. The court does not at this stage automatically set a trial date or a period within which the trial will take place.

Disadvantages of civil courts

Too expensive

Research carried out for Lord Woolf's review found that one side's costs exceeded the amount in dispute in over 40% of claims for under £12,500. The survey concluded that the simplest cases often incurred the highest costs in proportion to the value of the claim (see *Campbell* v *MGN*, 2004). In *Leigh and Baigent* v *Random House*, the writers of a novel claimed breach of copyright because similar themes appeared in *The Da Vinci Code*. They lost and had to pay their own legal costs of £800,000 plus Random House's legal costs of £1,100,000.

Because of the complexity of the civil courts procedure, lawyers are usually needed. High Court litigation is not for the inexperienced, so barristers draft the pleadings and advise on the evidence. To employ such legal expertise is expensive. The sheer length of civil proceedings also impacts on the costs.

Delays

The Civil Justice Review, set up in 1985, observed that the system was overstretched, and that the time between the incident that gave rise to the claim and the trial could be up to 3 years for County Courts and 5 years for the High Court. Research carried out for Lord Woolf found that the worst delays were in personal injury and medical negligence cases, which took a median time of 54 and 61 months respectively. The average waiting time for a County Court claim was 79 weeks.

Injustice

Usually, an out-of-court settlement is negotiated before the litigants ever reach trial. For every 9,000 personal injury cases commenced, only 300 reach trial. Outside such cases, for every 100,000 writs issued before 1999, fewer than 300 came to trial. There are advantages to reaching such a settlement — a quick end to the dispute and a significant reduction in costs — but it can equally be argued that the high number of such settlements creates injustice because the parties often hold unequal bargaining positions.

> **Examiner tip**
> Ensure that you learn both the financial limits and the courts for each of these three tracks — many marks are lost by students who fail to remember these straightforward facts. Remember that a question on these different tracks may also be set in Law 02 papers.

> **Knowledge check 30**
> What are the reasons for the high costs of civil trials?

Finally, the rules on payments in court increase the unfairness of the pre-trial procedures. As Professor Zander observed, the rule is 'highly favourable' to the defendant, and puts pressure on the claimant to accept an offer.

The adversarial process

Many problems result from the adversarial process, which encourages tactical manoeuvring rather than cooperation. It would be far simpler, and therefore cheaper, for each side to state precisely what it alleges in the pleadings, disclose all the documents it holds, and give the other side copies of its witness statements.

Unwanted publicity

Courts are open to the public and the press. This means that private (and possibly, embarrassing) details will be widely reported as occurred in the divorce action between Sir Paul McCartney and Heather Mills, during which the judge was very critical of Heather Mills, saying that she exaggerated and made fraudulent claims.

Advantages of civil courts

While most students are able to state the problems of civil courts in terms of delay, expense and formality, comparatively few can explain the advantages that these courts have over any other form of dispute resolution.

Compulsory process

There is no other process by which you can effectively compel the other side to come to a forum to resolve a dispute. The other party could, of course, decline to lodge a defence or even to appear in court, but in that case, a default judgement would be issued against it.

Formality of procedures

Rules of evidence, disclosure and legal argument all ensure a fair process. This process is supervised by a judge, who is a trained and qualified expert in the law and legal processes.

Appeal process

No other dispute-resolution process allows for appeals. Even with the introduction of Upper Tier tribunals, it is easier to appeal from one court to a higher court. This is also the position with arbitration. Appeals from arbitration can only be made to the High Court on a point of law and such appeals are rare.

Legal aid

Although civil legal aid has been greatly reduced in recent years, particularly as a result of reforms in the **Access to Justice Act 1999**, it is still more widely available for court litigation than for any alternative. It is also true that lawyers are more likely to litigate on a conditional fee basis in court than in tribunals, arbitration or mediation.

Law making and development

Only courts, especially the Court of Appeal and the Supreme Court, can make and develop legal rules through the doctrine of precedent. Any decision given in arbitration, and even in tribunals, applies only to the case in question. It is essential, in the areas of business and taxation, for companies and individuals to understand the relevant legal rules, and to be able to challenge these through the appellate system to allow the law to develop.

Enforcement of decision

Courts have greater powers to enforce their decisions than any other dispute-resolution agency. Court decisions can be enforced by sending in the bailiffs, attachment of earnings order, charging order, etc.

Knowledge check 31

List the advantages of civil courts.

The civil justice system after April 1999

On 26 April 1999, new Civil Procedure Rules (CPR) came into force. The reformed rules aim to eliminate unnecessary cost, delay and complexity. The general approach of Lord Woolf is reflected in his statement: 'If "time and money are no object" was the right approach in the past, it certainly is not today.'

The first rule of the CPR sets the overriding objective of the whole system — that the rules should enable the courts to deal with cases 'justly'. This objective prevails over all other rules in the case of a conflict.

Dealing with a case 'justly' involves the following factors:
- ensuring the parties are on an equal footing
- saving expense
- ensuring 'proportionality' in the way the case is dealt with in terms of the value of the claim, the importance and complexity of the case and the financial position of each party
- ensuring that it is dealt with expeditiously and fairly
- allotting to it an appropriate share of the court's resources

The emphasis of the new rules is on avoiding litigation by means of pre-trial settlements. Litigation is to be viewed as a last resort; the court has a continuing obligation to encourage and facilitate settlement.

Alternative dispute resolution (ADR)

This is greatly encouraged and actively promoted by the court. There is a general statement in the Civil Procedure Rules that the court's duty to further the overriding objective by active case management includes both encouraging the parties to use an ADR procedure and facilitating the use of that procedure.

An excellent example of the 'pressure' to make ADR successful was provided by the case of *Dunnett* v *Railtrack plc* (2002). Railtrack, which won the case, was not awarded its costs because it had 'turned down flat' an offer of ADR after the court had suggested that this would be the best way to resolve the dispute between the parties. As the claim by Mrs Dunnett was only for £9,000 and the legal costs of taking the case

Knowledge check 32

What is the importance of the decision in *Dunnett* v *Railtrack*?

up to the Court of Appeal amounted to more than £100,000, Railtrack made an expensive mistake.

Recently, the Court of Appeal has delivered important guidance on the use of mediation and ADR in personal injury litigation. In the consolidated appeals of *Halsey* v *Milton Keynes General NHS Trust* and *Steel* v *Joy and Halliday* (2004), the court ruled on when it is appropriate to penalise a party who refuses mediation.

Summary

County Courts:
- specific local jurisdiction
- all contract and tort actions under £50,000
- other cases include bankruptcy, tax cases, land disputes and granting repossession orders

The High Court has three divisions — Queen's Bench, Chancery and Family.

The Court of Appeal hears appeals mostly from the High Court.

The Supreme Court hears most appeals taken from the Court of Appeal.

Case management:
- small claims — actions under £5,000 (up to £1,000 for personal injury cases); small claims procedure in County Court
- fast-track — actions between £5,000 and £25,000 heard in County Court
- multi-track — actions over £25,000 up to £50,000 in County Court; actions over £50,000 in High Court

Alternatives to courts

Tribunals

The past century has seen considerable growth in the potential for disputes between individuals, groups and state agencies. The expansion of agencies created for the implementation of state interventionist policies, as in the field of welfare provision, has created, in turn, the potential for disputes between individuals and social welfare officials, and between property owners and planning authorities. Frequently, the legislation that established the machinery for implementing such policies has also set up the institutional framework within which disputes in particular fields are to be resolved. It is significant that in many such cases, the dispute-solving mechanisms adopted have not been ordinary courts of law, but rather specialised tribunals.

If all disputes created under the weight of social legislation had to be settled in ordinary courts, the court system would collapse under the enormous workload. Furthermore, the courts are, for many of these cases, inappropriate for dealing with the dispute.

In order to provide a system for resolving disputes without the trappings of law courts, various governments have introduced, through legislation, a network of administrative tribunals designed to provide instant justice cheaply, efficiently and with minimum delay and formality. These tribunals comprise not highly paid judges but panels made up of a chairperson, who is usually legally qualified, and two non-legally qualified people who have expertise in the particular field over which the tribunal has jurisdiction. In all, there are about 70 different types of tribunal, hearing over 1 million cases each year. In England and Wales, more people take cases to tribunals than to any other part of the justice system.

Knowledge check 33

Who will usually form a tribunal panel?

Tribunals are now regulated under the **Tribunals, Courts and Enforcement Act 2007** which has the following aims:
- making sure that all tribunals are independent of the government
- speeding up the delivery of justice
- making processes easier for the public to understand and more user friendly
- creating a clearer structure

Structure of tribunals

There is now a **First Tier Tribunal** which hears new cases. It is divided into six chambers including:
- the Social Entitlement Chamber which deals with social security and child support, as well as criminal injuries compensation
- the Health, Education and Social Care Chamber which deals with mental health and special educational needs and disability
- the Immigration and Asylum Chamber

Cases are decided by a judge and two lay people with relevant expertise (the panel). Procedures are more flexible and informal than court and the panel try to help by asking questions to find out all the information they need. They are inquisitorial rather than adversarial. They are usually held in private and legal aid is not available. Instead of all the tribunals having different rules, all chambers follow the same procedures and these are designed to make it easier for people to represent themselves.

The 2007 Act also established an **Upper Tribunal** to hear appeals from the First Tier Tribunals — there are four separate chambers including the Administrative Appeals Chamber and the Immigration and Asylum Chamber.

Advantages of tribunals

Speed

Tribunal cases come to court quickly and are often dealt with in a day. It is usually possible to specify the exact date and time when a case will be heard, thus minimising time wasting for the parties. In some tribunals, e.g. employment tribunals, it is common for a process of mediation or conciliation to be used to deal with the case initially. This often results in a solution without the need for a full hearing, which in turn saves further time and expense.

Cost

Tribunals do not usually charge fees, and each party pays its own costs, rather than the loser having to pay everything. The simpler procedures of tribunals mean that legal representation is unnecessary, and costs are therefore reduced.

Informality

The level of formality varies between different tribunals, but, as a general rule, wigs are not worn, the strict rules of evidence do not apply and attempts are made to create an unintimidating atmosphere. This is important when individuals are representing themselves.

Knowledge check 34

Why do tribunals play such an important part in dispute resolution?

Examiner tip

Ensure that in any question on the work of tribunals, you do not confuse tribunals and courts — they are very separate.

Flexibility

Although tribunals aim to apply principles consistently, they do not operate strict rules of precedent and are therefore able to respond more flexibly than courts. Few of their decisions are reported formally.

Specialisation

Tribunal members already have expertise in the relevant subject area, and through sitting on tribunals they are able to build up a depth of knowledge that judges in ordinary courts could not hope to match.

Reduces pressure on courts

Without tribunals, ordinary courts would be swamped with cases, and delays would be many times worse than they are at present.

Knowledge check 35

Why is taking a case to a tribunal usually much cheaper than going to court?

Privacy

Tribunals may, in some circumstances, meet in private, so that individuals are not obliged to have their problems aired in public.

Disadvantages of tribunals

Lack of openness

The fact that some tribunals are held in private can lead to suspicion about the fairness of their decisions.

Unavailability of legal aid

Full civil legal aid is available for only three tribunals — prison disciplinary, mental health and the parole board. Although assistance in case preparation is available under the legal advice and assistance scheme, this does not cover representation.

Tribunals are designed to obviate the need for legal representation, but in many cases the ordinary claimant faces an opponent with access to the best representation, e.g. an employer or a government department, and this places him or her at a serious disadvantage. Even though the procedures are generally informal compared with litigation, the average person is likely to be out of his or her depth. Research by Genn and Genn in 1989 found that much of the law with which tribunals are concerned is complex, and adjudication processes are sometimes highly technical.

Knowledge check 36

Why, despite the informality of tribunals, can it be a disadvantage for one party not to be legally represented?

There is, however, some dispute about the desirability of such representation involving lawyers. Although in certain cases this is the most appropriate form of representation, there are fears that the introduction of lawyers could affect the aims of speed and informality.

Lack of independence

The requirement of independence is compromised by the fact that members of some tribunals are appointed by the minister on whose decisions they have to adjudicate. Although there is no evidence that this results in bias, it is difficult for such tribunals to achieve the appearance of impartiality. However, the **Tribunals, Courts and Enforcement Act 2007** has laid down the aim that all tribunals are independent of the government.

Lack of reasons

Reasons for decisions are not always given, although this has been strongly recommended by the Court of Appeal and is a requirement of the **Human Rights Act 1998**.

Too complex

The 1979 Royal Commission on Legal Services (the Benson Commission) recommended a review of tribunal procedures, with a view to simplifying the process so that applicants could as far as possible represent themselves. However, if anything, tribunal procedures have become more legalistic.

Problems with control

Considered together, tribunals vary widely and make thousands of decisions each year in different types of case. It is not easy to supervise this diversity. The Upper Tier appellate tribunals should address this particular problem.

Non-adversarial procedures

Alternative dispute resolution (ADR) schemes have been in use in the USA, Australia, Canada and New Zealand for many years, and have been endorsed by the current Lord Chancellor in the light of major criticisms of the civil justice system and the pressures on legal aid. A court decision offers certainty and finality (subject to rights of appeal), but such decisions are often outweighed by delay, cost and the stress of undertaking litigation.

ADR attempts to involve the client in the process of resolving the dispute. It does not rely on an adversarial approach but rather on reaching an agreement. Each case is decided on its merits without reference to previous cases, and the common ground between the parties should be emphasised, rather than focusing on points of disagreement. ADR offers a confidential process, and the outcome will not be published without the consent of both parties. Resolution of a dispute can be fast and straightforward, and hearing times and places are at the agreement of both parties.

Arbitration

Arbitration may be defined as the determination of a dispute by an impartial person (rather than a court) after hearing both sides in a judicial manner. It is an increasingly popular way of resolving disputes, where both parties voluntarily agree to an independent third party making a decision in their case. It has been described as 'privatised litigation with the judge and venue paid for by the parties'. The process is governed by the **Arbitration Act 1996**.

The arbitrator is usually chosen by the parties and may be a businessperson or lawyer or someone with technical knowledge, e.g. an engineer or architect, according to the basis of the dispute. The date, place and time, the method of arbitration and the powers of the arbitrator are all matters for the parties to decide in consultation with the arbitrator.

There are different types of arbitration:

- **Small claims court.** Although the small claims court takes place as part of the jurisdiction of the County Court, the procedure followed is that of arbitration. The district judge is not bound to adopt strict court rules of evidence and procedure, and acts in effect as an arbitrator. The financial limit is £5,000 and most cases involve debt recovery or consumer problems.
- **Consumer arbitration.** The Office of Fair Trading (OFT) has in recent years encouraged and approved many arbitration schemes set up by trade associations to resolve consumer problems, e.g. the Association of British Travel Agents (ABTA).
- **Commercial arbitration.** The complexity of business contracts makes disputes likely. One way to limit the damage and expense caused by such disputes is for the parties to go to arbitration rather than to the courts. Arbitration is more likely to maintain business relations between the parties than the more adversarial court process. For these reasons, many business contracts contain a *Scott* v *Avery* clause, whereby disputes must first be referred to arbitration.

Knowledge check 37

What is a *Scott* v *Avery* clause?

Advantages of arbitration

- Parties retain more control over arbitration than over a court case, where the control is effectively exercised by lawyers and the judge. The parties themselves choose the arbitrator, the procedure to be adopted, the time and place and the length of arbitration. They can also agree to limit the arbitrator's powers.
- The proceedings are held in private — an important consideration for commercial disputes.
- Arbitration is usually quicker and cheaper than court proceedings. This is because having agreed to resolve the dispute by this process, it is in the interest of both parties to set up the arbitration quickly.
- In addition to having legal knowledge of the issue in dispute, an arbitrator will also be an expert in that area.

Disadvantages of arbitration

- There is no legal aid available. It should be noted, of course, that legal aid has been sharply reduced for much court-based litigation.
- Opportunity to appeal is limited.
- There may be difficulty in enforcing awards.
- There may be an imbalance between parties where only one party will have legal representation but not the other, e.g. consumer against company.
- As with all forms of consensual ADR, if the parties' positions are entrenched arbitration does not offer a realistic possibility of dispute resolution.

Knowledge check 38

What are the advantages of arbitration?

Mediation

Mediation is an informal procedure that assists disputing parties in their negotiations. It involves an independent, neutral third party acting as a go-between to facilitate cooperation and agreement. The mediator will often discuss the disputed matter with each party in separate rooms. Where the relationship between the parties needs to be preserved, as in family disputes or those involving commercial matters, mediation ensures that the relationship is not soured as it would be by litigation. Mediation is a voluntary process and, should it fail, the parties will have preserved their positions. It also allows the parties to feel in control.

In the UK, commercial mediation is promoted and organised by companies such as International Resolution Europe Ltd and the Centre for Dispute Resolution, founded in 1990 under the auspices of the Confederation of British Industry. Mediation in family disputes is available from the National Association of Family Mediation and Conciliation Services, which offers support to those who wish to conduct their own negotiations and only refer to lawyers in an advisory capacity.

Conciliation

Conciliation falls somewhere between arbitration and mediation, the former being the most formal, the latter the least formal. The conciliator offers a non-binding opinion, which may lead to a settlement.

ACAS offers a conciliation scheme in industrial disputes, which can be used in tribunal cases. The employer and the employee both send copies of their arguments to the ACAS representative who will be an expert in employment law and who will offer to act as a conciliator in the dispute. The parties do not meet, but the conciliator speaks to the employer and the employee separately, usually over the telephone.

Most of the bodies offering mediation services will also offer conciliation as well, such as the **National Association of Family Mediation and Conciliation Services.**

> **Examiner tip**
> If a question gives you a choice between explaining mediation or conciliation, choose mediation — there is much more material and examples for this.

Advantages of mediation and conciliation

- **Cost.** It is likely to be cheaper than using a court or tribunal because you probably will not need to use lawyers.
- **Flexibility.** Courts and tribunals have fixed hearings and procedures. The informality and relaxed nature of conciliation/mediation/negotiation contrasts with the complex and intimidating experience of being in court.
- **Preserves relationships and recognises parties' interests.** You are more likely to end up with a 'win, win' situation. The problem with courts and tribunals is that they tend to be adversarial with winners and losers. Mediation/conciliation/negotiation is based on compromise so that the parties are less likely to feel embittered by the outcome.

Disadvantages of mediation and conciliation

- **Not legally binding.** Mediation/conciliation/negotiation works through compromise and agreement. There is no authority figure like a judge to make a decision which the parties have to accept. Also there is no mechanism for forcing the parties to stick to what they have agreed. This may result in a party being forced to go to court anyway, feeling that they have wasted their time using ADR.

- **No equality of arms.** A judge in court can make a decision based on the merits of the case put forward by each party, but because mediation/conciliation/negotiation is informal and based on compromise it can allow a wealthier party or one that is in a stronger bargaining position to force an unfavourable settlement on the weaker party.
- **Not possible if positions are 'entrenched'.** Often one party might be unwilling to compromise or feel angry and hostile to the other party. This makes it very difficult to use mediation, conciliation or negotiation. Disputes between neighbours can often be very bitter — for example, an argument between neighbours over a tiny strip of land actually went to court. Also couples who are divorcing can often be very hostile to each other and unwilling to compromise.

Negotiation

This is the most basic and informal of all the ADR processes and is usually the first method to be used. It involves the parties communicating directly with each other to try to reach agreement. The communication may be by any method, for example face to face, on the telephone or by e-mail. They may negotiate directly or through their lawyers.

Any kind of dispute can be settled by negotiation, but to be successful it must focus on the issues rather than personalities. Low-key disputes, for example between a householder and a tradesman like an electrician or plumber or between neighbours, are often settled by negotiation, but it is also used to settle disputes between large companies. There are no costs involved in negotiation unless lawyers are used.

Conclusion

The aim of ADR is to facilitate settlement, whereas the aim of litigation is to obtain judgement, but note that judges are increasingly becoming involved with ADR, and barristers and solicitors too.

Examiner tip

Be sure to read questions on different forms of ADR carefully. Many marks are lost because students confuse the different types — arbitration, mediation and conciliation. Read examiner reports to learn from and avoid these common mistakes.

Summary

Tribunals

Tribunals are now regulated under the **Tribunals, Courts and Enforcement Act 2007**. It has the following aims:

- making sure that all tribunals are independent of the government
- speeding up the delivery of justice
- making processes easier for the public to understand and more user friendly
- creating a clearer structure

The First Tier Tribunal:

- This is divided into six chambers.
- They are inquisitorial. They are usually held in private and legal aid is not available.
- The 2007 Act also established an Upper Tribunal to hear appeals from the First Tier Tribunals.

Advantages of tribunals include:

- speed
- cost
- informality
- flexibility
- specialisation
- reduces pressure on courts
- awareness of policy
- privacy

Disadvantages of tribunals include:

- lack of openness
- unavailability of legal aid
- lack of independence
- lack of reasons
- too complex

- lack of accessibility
- problems with control

Non-adversarial procedures

These include arbitration, mediation, conciliation and negotiation.

Arbitration may be defined as the determination of a dispute by an impartial person after hearing both sides in a judicial manner. It is governed by the **Arbitration Act 1996**. There are different types of arbitration:

- small claims court
- consumer arbitration
- commercial arbitration

Advantages of arbitration include:

- parties retain more control over arbitration than over a court case
- held in private
- usually quicker and cheaper than court proceedings
- arbitrator will be an expert in that area

Disadvantages of arbitration include:

- no legal aid available
- limited appeal opportunities
- difficulty in enforcing awards
- possible imbalance between parties

- if the parties' positions are entrenched, arbitration does not offer a realistic possibility of dispute resolution

Mediation is an informal procedure that assists disputing parties in their negotiations. It involves an independent, neutral third party acting as a go-between to facilitate cooperation and agreement.

Conciliation falls somewhere between arbitration and mediation, the former being the most formal, the latter the least formal.

Advantages of mediation and conciliation include:

- cost
- flexibility
- preserves relationships and recognises parties' interests

Disadvantages of mediation and conciliation include:

- not legally binding
- no equality of arms
- not possible if positions are 'entrenched'

Negotiation is the most basic and informal of all the ADR processes and is usually the first method to be used. It involves the parties communicating directly with each other to try to reach agreement. There are no costs involved in negotiation unless lawyers are used.

Criminal courts and lay people

Criminal courts

Classification of offences

There are three different classes of criminal offence:

- **summary** — minor offences that can only be tried by Magistrates' Courts, e.g. motoring offences
- **either-way** — offences that may be tried either by magistrates or in a Crown Court before a judge and jury, e.g. theft
- **indictable** — serious offences that can only be tried in a Crown Court before a judge and jury, e.g. murder

The Magistrates' Court

The Magistrates' Court is the 'workhorse of the criminal justice system' and is responsible for hearing over 1 million cases each year. All summary offences and the majority of either-way offences are tried by Magistrates' Courts. Within these courts are the youth courts, which have the jurisdiction to try all offences charged against those aged from 10 to 17 (excluding murder, which can only be tried in a Crown Court).

Appeals are made to the Queen's Bench Division of the High Court on a point of law by way of case stated, or to the Crown Court against sentence or conviction.

The Crown Court

Although the Crown Court acts as an appeal court, hearing cases from Magistrates' Courts, its main jurisdiction is to hear all indictable offences (such as murder, rape and robbery) and the more serious either-way offences, where jurisdiction has been declined by magistrates or where the defendant has elected to be tried on indictment by a judge sitting with a jury.

The Court of Appeal (Criminal Division)

This is presided over by the Lord Chief Justice. Three judges make up the panel that hears appeals, usually a Lord Justice of Appeal accompanied by two senior High Court judges from the Queen's Bench Division.

Appeals may be made to this court by defendants against sentence or conviction from the Crown Court, provided leave to appeal has been granted. In appeals against sentence, the Court of Appeal may confirm or reduce the sentence imposed at trial.

The principal grounds for appealing against conviction are that the original conviction is 'unsafe or unsatisfactory', new evidence not available at the time of trial has come to light, or there has been a material irregularity in the course of the trial. The court can uphold the original conviction, quash it (i.e. overturn it and release the defendant), substitute a lower-level conviction (e.g. a manslaughter conviction where the original conviction was for murder) or order a retrial.

Knowledge check 39

What are the powers of the Court of Appeal (Criminal Division) in dealing with appeals against: (a) sentence and (b) conviction?

Appeals by the Attorney General

Under s.35 of the **Criminal Justice Act 1988**, the Attorney General, acting on behalf of the Crown Prosecution Service, can, with the leave of the court, appeal to the Court of Appeal against 'an unduly lenient sentence'.

The Attorney General can also refer a case to the Court of Appeal following an acquittal in the Crown Court, which he or she has reason to believe was the result of an error in law made by the judge in his or her directions to the jury. The purpose of such a referral is to verify the correct legal rule. The defendant, having been acquitted, is not identified in the citation, which is simply listed as 'Attorney General's Reference No... of [year]', and whatever decision on the law is made by the Court of Appeal, the acquittal is not affected in any way.

Juries

The jury system was imported into Britain after the Norman conquest, though its early functions were quite different from those it fulfils today.

A major milestone in the history of the jury was *Bushell*'s case (1670), where it was finally established that the jury members were the sole judges of fact, had the right to give a verdict according to their conscience and could not be penalised for taking a view of the facts opposed to that of the judge.

Juries, although important in our system of criminal justice, take part in fewer than 1% of all criminal trials — over 96% of criminal trials are conducted in Magistrates' Courts, and approximately 70% of defendants in Crown Courts plead guilty. A further proportion of defendants are found not guilty by means of 'directed acquittals', where the trial judge instructs the jury as a matter of law to return a formal verdict of 'not guilty'.

Examiner tip

This topic is one of the most popular examination choices — but remember that you may be asked questions on both magistrates' and criminal courts.

Selection of jurors

Before 1972, only people who owned a home over a certain rateable value were eligible for jury service. The Morris Committee in 1965 estimated that 78% of those on the electoral register did not qualify for jury service, and 95% of women were ineligible. The current qualifications for jury service are detailed in the **Juries Act 1974** as amended by the **Criminal Justice Act 1988** which provides that potential jury members must be:

- aged between 18 and 70 years
- on the electoral register
- resident in the UK, Channel Islands or Isle of Man for at least 5 years since the age of 13

The jury summoning officer arranges for potential jurors' names to be picked at random from the electoral register by the Central Jury Summoning Bureau. From those selected (who are not excused or do not have jury service deferred), 20 are chosen randomly by the jury usher for the particular trial. These potential jurors — the 'jury in waiting' — are then told the name of the defendant and asked if they know him or her. If they do, they leave the court and return to the jury pool to be used for another trial. At court, a final random selection takes place and 12 jurors are selected to form a jury. However, some people are either excluded or excused from jury service on the following grounds:

- **Disqualification** — those with a criminal conviction who have received a custodial or community sentence within the last 10 years are disqualified. Imprisonment for 5 years or more results in life-time disqualification. Offenders on bail are also disqualified.
- **Ineligibility** — under the **Criminal Justice Act 2003** the only people ineligible for jury service are those suffering from a mental illness who are resident in a hospital or have regular treatment by a medical practitioner.
- **Excusal as of right** — with the exception of those aged between 65 and 70, this category was abolished by the **Criminal Justice Act 2003**. This change has the effect of enabling clergymen, lawyers, police officers and even judges to become jurors.

What are the key criteria for jury selection and what changes were introduced by the Criminal Justice Act 2003?

- **Excusal at the court's discretion** — those with limited understanding of English, students doing public examinations, parents with childcare commitments/problems or people with prior commitments such as booked holidays may be excused from jury service. However, in such cases it is more likely that jury service will be deferred than cancelled. Full-time members of the armed forces may be excused if their commanding officer certifies that their absence from duty would be prejudicial to the efficiency of the service.

Jury challenging and vetting

In the UK, challenging a juror is a rare event, but there are three main ways in which it can occur:

(1) Prosecution can use '**Stand by for the Crown**' without giving a reason, although the Attorney General announced in 1988 that this right would only be used to remove a 'manifestly unsuitable' juror or to remove a juror in a terrorist/security trial where jury vetting has been authorised.

(2) Defence can challenge '**for cause**', which, in terms of a Practice Note issued by the Lord Chief Justice in 1973, may not include race, religion, political beliefs or occupation. A successful challenge is therefore only likely to occur where the juror is personally known.

(3) Both parties may challenge the whole jury panel — '**challenge to the array**' — on the grounds that the summoning officer is biased or has acted improperly. This happens rarely.

What are the three ways in which a jury may be challenged?

The process of **jury vetting** is conducted by the prosecution with the written permission of the Attorney General and involves checking the list of potential jurors to see if anyone appears 'unsuitable'.

The function of the jury

Jurors have to weigh up the evidence and decide what the true facts of the case are. The judge directs them as to what the relevant law is, and they must then apply that law to the facts that they have found and thereby reach a verdict. There is a partnership between the judge, who acts as 'master of the law', and the jury, which is 'master of the facts'.

Criminal cases

Juries are used in all serious criminal cases: that is, indictable offences tried at Crown Court. The jury has the sole responsibility for determining guilt. Since the **Criminal Justice Act 1967**, majority verdicts are possible (a minimum of ten out of 12 must agree).

During the trial, after being sworn in, jurors are present to hear all the evidence put forward in the case by the prosecution and defence counsel. Notes may be taken and jurors have the opportunity to question witnesses through the judge.

At the end of the case for the defence and after the closing speeches of counsel, the judge summarises the evidence in the case and directs the jury on relevant legal issues. In complicated cases, the judge also provides a structured set of questions to assist the jury in its deliberations. The jury retires to a private room, where it chooses a foreperson to present its verdict. If the jury has not returned with a unanimous verdict after a minimum period of 2 hours 10 minutes, the judge may recall it and advise that a majority verdict may be made under the **Criminal Justice Act 1967** (about 20% of convictions each year are given by such verdicts).

Advantages of jury trial

Public participation

Juries allow the ordinary citizen to take part in the administration of justice, so that verdicts are seen to be those of society rather than of the judicial system. This satisfies the constitutional tradition of judgement by one's peers. Lord Denning described jury service as giving 'ordinary folk their finest lesson in citizenship'.

A survey commissioned by the Bar Council and the Law Society found that:

- over 80% of those questioned were likely to have more confidence in juries than in other players in the justice system
- over 80% thought that juries were likely to reflect their views and values
- 85% trusted juries to reach the right decision
- 85% thought that juries improved the quality of the justice system

These findings have particular importance when one considers the background of magistrates, who continue to be predominantly white and middle class.

Layman's equity

Because juries have the ultimate right to find defendants innocent or guilty, it is argued that they act as a check on officialdom and protect against unjust or oppressive prosecution by reflecting a community's sense of justice. By 'bending the law', juries, unlike judges and magistrates, have the power to acquit a defendant where the law demands a guilty verdict. There are several well-known cases of juries using this right to find according to their consciences, often in cases dealing with issues of political and moral controversy, e.g. *R v Ponting* (1985), *R v Kronlid* (1996) and *R v Owen* (1992). The importance of this aspect of the jury's involvement in criminal justice is difficult to assess. In high-profile cases such as *Ponting*, it can be a valuable statement of public feeling to those in authority, but it cannot always be relied upon.

Better 'decision making'

On the key issue of deciding guilt or innocence, it can be argued that even criminal cases that involve complex issues of law come down to a consideration of essential facts, e.g. identification, witness credibility and dishonesty (in a theft case). Such matters are more likely to be decided correctly as a result of discussion between unbiased and legally unqualified people than by a single judge. Individual jurors form different impressions about the truthfulness of various witnesses and the legal arguments submitted by opposing counsel.

Examiner tip

Note how much explanation is provided here as to the function or role of juries in criminal trials — not just simply 'deciding whether or not the defendant is guilty or not'. Another key issue is that of majority verdicts and the need to refer to the statutory authority which enabled these to be given.

Examiner tip

This particular argument is important because it enables you to explain cases.

Disadvantages of juries

Lack of competence

Particular concern has been expressed about the average jury's understanding of complex fraud cases. In 1986, the Roskill Committee concluded that trial by random jury was not a satisfactory way of achieving justice in such cases, since many jurors were 'out of their depth'. However, this Committee could not find accurate evidence of a higher proportion of acquittals in complex fraud cases than in any other kind of case. In a recent serious fraud trial — R v *Rayment and Others,* which collapsed in 2005 after many months and a cost of over £60 million — an inquiry conducted by HM Chief Inspector of the Crown Prosecution Service, Stephen Wooler, concluded that 'a better monument to the endeavours of juries in this country or a better justification for the jury system would be hard to find'. In a research study by Professor Sally Lloyd-Bostock, it was stated that the jury 'did indeed have a good grasp of the evidence'.

However, the New Zealand Law Commission, which was able under its own rules to carry out more detailed research on how real juries had performed in trials, reported in 1999 that jurors admitted to having serious problems in understanding key legal terms such as 'intention' and 'beyond reasonable doubt'. Problems were also encountered with concentration levels in lengthy trials, particularly with oral evidence.

Although both Conservative and Labour governments have tried to remove jury trials for fraud cases, such has been the strength of arguments by lawyers and judges that no changes have been made.

Jury nobbling

Despite the introduction of majority verdicts in the **Criminal Justice Act 1967**, it is believed that jury nobbling remains a major weakness. Jury nobbling is an attempt made by means of threats or bribery to 'persuade' a juror to return a 'not-guilty' verdict. In 1982, several Old Bailey trials had to be stopped because of attempted nobbling. In 1984, jurors in the *Brinks Mat* trial had to have police protection to and from the court, and their telephone calls were intercepted. A new criminal offence of intimidating or threatening to harm jurors was introduced in the **Criminal Procedure and Investigation Act 1996** to try to give additional protection to juries.

Bias

Ingman suggests that jurors may be biased for or against certain groups, e.g. the police. However, in a group of 12 jurors, it is likely that individual bias will be cancelled out. This issue of potential bias was the basis of an appeal in the cases of R v *Abdroikov,* R v *Green* and R v *Williamson* in 2007. In these cases, because of the changes made in jury selection in the **Criminal Justice Act 2003**, one of the jurors was a police officer, in the second the victim was a police officer and the police officer on the jury was from the same local police background, and in the third, a juror was an experienced Crown Prosecutor. Although there was no evidence of actual bias in any of these cases, the House of Lords held that in the police victim case and the CPS prosecutor case, a reasonable onlooker would conclude that justice had not been seen to be done because of the proximity of the jurors to the issues to be decided. These convictions were quashed.

Cost

One argument against juries is that jury trials in the Crown Court are more expensive than trials in the Magistrates' Court. However, by far the greatest expense in the Crown Court is the cost of lawyers, judges and other court personnel. Most criminal trials last no more than a day, and the maximum jury cost for that is only £500.

Difficulties with appeals

When judges sit alone, their judgement consists of a detailed and explicit finding of fact. When there is a jury, the verdict is returned unexplained as, under s.8 of the **Contempt of Court Act 1981**, jury deliberations are secret.

Media pressure

In serious cases where there is a great deal of media publicity, it has been argued that juries are more likely than judges to be 'swayed' by this publicity. Further problems have arisen as shown in two recent examples. At Luton Crown Court in July 2011, one of the jurors, Theodora Dallas, was charged with contempt of court after she defied a direction by the judge and researched the internet to discover the past criminal record of the defendant. In 2011 Joanne Fraill was sentenced to 8 months in prison for contacting a defendant in a drugs trial via Facebook.

> **Examiner tip**
> As with advantages, ensure you write 'paragraph' answers which focus on the key issue of jury competence where there are contrasting points of view.

Magistrates

About 30,000 lay magistrates try more than 2 million cases a year — over 96% of all criminal cases — while about 130 District Judges (Magistrates' Courts) with a 7-year general advocacy qualification (formerly called stipendiaries) are appointed by the queen on the recommendation of the Lord Chancellor.

Selection and appointment

Under the **Justices of the Peace Act 1997**, lay magistrates are appointed by the Lord Chancellor on the advice of county local advisory committees. Members of these committees, mostly drawn from the magistracy, are appointed by the Lord Chancellor. Nowadays candidates must make a formal application — either in response to an advertisement or by making an enquiry through the government website.

The only qualifications for appointment to the magistracy are that the applicants must be aged between 18 and 65 and they are expected to live or work within the local justice area to which they are allocated. For many years Lord Chancellors would not appoint people under the age of 27 as it was felt that they did not possess the necessary experience. However, in recent years a number of younger magistrates have been appointed, including a 21-year-old disc jockey in Horsham and a 19-year-old law student in Pontefract.

Applicants must be able to devote, on average, half a day a week to the task, for which only expenses and a small loss of earnings allowance are given. Certain people

Knowledge check 42

Including those excluded, what are the qualifications needed to become a magistrate?

are excluded from the magistracy: police officers, traffic wardens, probation officers and members of their immediate families; members of the armed forces; those with certain criminal convictions; and undischarged bankrupts.

In 1998, the Lord Chancellor revised the procedures for appointing lay magistrates, aiming to make the criteria open and clear. A job description was introduced, which states that the six key qualities defining the personal suitability of candidates are:

- good character
- understanding and communication
- social awareness
- maturity and sound temperament
- sound judgement
- commitment and reliability

The advisory committee arranges interviews for shortlisted candidates after their references have been checked. There are two interviews: the first examines the candidate's character; the second, comprising sentencing and trial exercises, assesses the candidate's judgement. After the interviews, potential appointees are reviewed by the local advisory committee to ensure that a 'balanced bench' can be achieved in terms of age, gender, ethnic background and occupation. The committee submits its recommendations to the Lord Chancellor, who usually accepts them and makes the appointment. The final stage is the 'swearing-in' of new magistrates by a senior circuit judge.

Magistrates can be removed by the Lord Chancellor at any time, but only in cases where an individual is deemed to have misbehaved or acted in a way that is inconsistent with the office. Magistrates usually have to retire at 70.

Training

Training is organised by the Judicial Studies Board and is carried out by a team of legal advisers, supported by appropriate professionals such as psychiatrists, probation officers, lawyers and judges. On appointment, all magistrates receive an intensive induction course to familiarise them with court procedures and the theory and practice of sentencing. Since 1998, the amount of training has intensified, with the appointment of experienced magistrates as mentors who support the training and development organised under the Magistrates National Training Initiative (MNTI 2) programme. New magistrates are assessed within 2 years of their appointment to ensure they have acquired the necessary competencies.

Examiner tip

Students rarely fully explain the training programme — often there is no reference to the specialist training provided for youth and family courts.

Magistrates who sit in youth courts or on family court panels receive additional training, as do magistrates who wish to become court chairpersons.

Criminal jurisdiction

Lay magistrates have four main functions in criminal cases:

(1) hearing applications for bail (**Bail Act 1976**) and legal aid

(2) trying all summary offences and the majority of 'either-way' offences; they are advised on points of law by legally qualified clerks, but they alone decide the facts, interpret the law and, where they convict, decide the sentence and any costs and compensation

(3) dealing with appeals: in ordinary appeals against conviction and/or sentence from the Magistrates' Courts to the Crown Court, magistrates (usually two) sit with a circuit judge

(4) dealing with requests for arrest and search warrants from the police

Youth court

The proceedings in the youth court are similar to but less formal than those in the adult courts. They are held in the presence of three magistrates and the justice's clerk. The magistrates concerned in youth courts must have received additional training and there must be a mixed-gender bench. A parent or guardian must be present, and the youth may be accompanied by a legal representative or social worker.

Unlike the adult court, the hearing is held in private and the defendant's name is not disclosed to the public unless it is in the public interest. If found guilty, the young person is either bound over or receives a deferred sentence, a community sentence or (only if he or she is over 15) a sentence of detention in a young offenders' institution.

Other sentences include a fine, an absolute or conditional discharge, an antisocial behaviour order (ASBO) or an attendance centre order (for 10–20-year-olds). A referral order is relevant only for first-time offenders who have pleaded guilty; it is set at between 3 and 12 months, depending on the seriousness of the offence.

Knowledge check 43

In what ways does the procedure in the youth court differ from an adult court?

Procedure for indictable offences

Section 51 of the **Crime and Disorder Act 1998** states that for indictable-only offences, adults appearing in the Magistrates' Court should 'be sent forthwith' to the Crown Court. Submissions of 'no case to answer' are now part of the pre-trial procedure at the Crown Court. This process removes the former committal powers of magistrates in such cases.

Powers of magistrates

The maximum term of imprisonment that can be imposed by magistrates is 6 months, unless there are two or more charges that can carry a term of imprisonment, in which case a total of 12 months can be imposed. The maximum fine that magistrates can impose is £5,000. In the youth court, magistrates have the power to sentence a young offender to 2 years' youth custody.

Justices' clerks and legal advisers

Because lay magistrates are not legally qualified and possess only an elementary knowledge of criminal law, it is the function of the justices' clerk or the legal adviser to sit in court with the magistrates' bench, to administer the court and to advise the justices on points of administrative and substantive law and on sentencing.

Note that in *R v Eccles Justices* (1989) the Queen's Bench divisional court ruled that the magistrates' decision could not stand because the legal adviser had acted outside his powers when he retired with the magistrates for 25 of the 30 minutes of their retirement from the courtroom. The suggestion was that he participated in the decision-making process.

District judges

District judges in Magistrates' Courts are legally qualified, paid judges, who have been barristers or solicitors for at least 7 years. They are appointed to courts in large cities or within a county. Retirement is at the age of 70, unless the Lord Chancellor permits an extension.

Advantages of the magistracy

Cost

Because lay magistrates are volunteers, the system is extremely cost-effective. In 2003/04, their expenses amounted to only £15 million — an average of £500 per magistrate. In 1989, the system cost about £200 million per year to run and brought in a total income of almost £270 million in fines.

Lay magistrates try the majority of criminal cases. To pay professional judges to deal with such an enormous caseload would be hugely expensive — at least £100 million per year in salaries alone, plus the cost of appointment and training — and it would take a long time to appoint and train the required number of legally qualified candidates.

Lay involvement

The true value of this is open to doubt because of the restricted social background of magistrates. However, because magistrates usually live within a reasonable distance of the court, this may provide them with a better-informed picture of local life than judges might have. A further important point is the diversity of magistrates: almost half of magistrates are female and around 8.5% are appointed from ethnic minorities.

Weight of numbers

The simple fact that magistrates usually sit in threes may make a balanced view more likely — in a real sense they sit as a 'mini-jury'.

Speed of bringing cases to court

Most defendants who have been arrested will appear before magistrates within 24 hours of arrest for a preliminary hearing. Even those defendants who are summoned to court will be tried within a few months. Crown Court trials often only start about a year after the defendant has been arrested and charged. After the 2011 riots that occurred in London and other cities, Magistrates' Courts sat overnight and on weekends to provide 'instant justice' which would not have been possible in Crown Courts.

Disadvantages of the magistracy

Inconsistency

There is considerable inconsistency in the decision making of different benches, particularly noticeable in the awards of legal aid and the types of sentence ordered. Research has confirmed that some benches are over ten times more likely to impose a custodial sentence than neighbouring benches for similar offences.

Examiner tip

As with juries, ensure that you avoid bullet-point answers — cost and lay involvement are the two key arguments in terms of advantages.

Bias towards the police

Police officers are frequent witnesses and become well known to magistrates. It has been argued that this results in an almost automatic tendency to believe police evidence. In *R* v *Bingham JJ ex parte Jowitt* (1974), a speeding case where the only evidence was that of the motorist and a policeman, the chairman of the bench said that where there was direct conflict between the defendant and the police 'my principle... has always been to believe the evidence of the police officer'. The conviction was quashed because of this remark, which was severely criticised.

'Cheap/amateur' justice argument

Because the chances of acquittal are substantially higher in the Crown Court than in the Magistrates' Court, the suspicion is created that the Crown Court is a fairer forum or even that magistrates are not as fair as they might be. It should be noted, however, that over 90% of defendants plead guilty in Magistrates' Courts, and the nature of most cases depends more on factual issues (e.g. drink-driving) than complex legal problems.

Increasing complexity of the law

Many crimes are being downgraded to summary offences, and new offences are being created. Sentencing has become more complex in recent years, with the introduction of curfew orders and ASBOs, for example. However, it should be noted that very few appeals against conviction or sentence are successful, signifying that despite their 'amateur' status, magistrates do a remarkably good job.

> **Examiner tip**
> As with advantages, write your answers in paragraphs. Focus on inconsistency in sentencing, possible bias towards the police and the 'cheap/amateur' justice issues.

Summary

Criminal Courts

- Classification of offences: summary, either-way or indictable.
- Magistrates' Courts: try all summary and most either-way offences.
- Youth court.
- Crown Court: hears all indictable offences with judge and jury; and more serious either-way offences. Also hears appeals against sentence or conviction from Magistrates' Courts.
- Court of Appeal (Criminal Division): hears appeals from Crown Court against sentence or conviction; also appeals by Attorney General against 'unduly lenient' sentences and 'reference' appeals.

Juries

- Selection: under **Juries Act 1974**, jurors must be aged 18–70, on the electoral register and resident in the UK for 5 years. Those disqualified include those with a criminal conviction and those on bail. Under **Criminal Justice Act 2003**, only those with mental illness are ineligible. Note jury challenges and vetting.
- Function: to return verdict of guilty or not guilty, having heard all the evidence and received legal directions from judge. Majority verdicts possible under **Criminal Justice Act 1967**.
- Advantages of juries:
  - public participation
  - layman's equity — note relevant cases
  - better decision making
- Disadvantages of juries:
  - lack of competence
  - jury nobbling
  - bias
  - cost
  - media pressure
  - difficulty with appeals

Magistrates

Selection, appointment and training:

- Under **Justices of the Peace Act 1997**, magistrates must be 18–65 and live locally, and possess six qualities laid down by Lord Chancellor — good character, maturity, commitment etc.
- Appointed by Lord Chancellor on recommendation of Advisory Committees which after two separate interviews consider need for 'balanced bench'.
- Training involves induction and sentencing.

Functions and powers include:

- bail and legal aid applications
- trial of all summary and most either-way offences
- search and arrest warrants
- appeals with circuit judge in Crown Court
- youth court
- sentencing: £5,000 fine and/or 6 months' imprisonment

Advantages of magistrates:

- cost
- lay involvement
- weight of numbers

Disadvantages of magistrates:

- inconsistency of sentencing
- bias
- 'cheap/amateur' justice
- increasing complexity of law

Legal professions

In England and Wales, there are two distinct legal professions — barristers and solicitors — and two 'subsidiary' professions — licensed conveyancers and legal executives.

Solicitors

Qualifications

Usually, solicitors have a university degree, but not necessarily a law degree. Any other degree or a non-qualifying law degree has to be followed by the Graduate Diploma in Law (GDL) — a 1-year full-time course, or 2 years part time. After the law degree or GDL, those wanting to become solicitors take the Legal Practice Course (LPC), and then undertake a 2-year training contract with a firm of solicitors, during which they have to complete a 20-day professional skills course. With these qualifications, individuals are entered onto the rolls of the Law Society and are entitled to practise as solicitors. After qualifying, solicitors have to continue their professional development by attending various courses.

While the majority of solicitors who qualify each year are graduates, it is possible to qualify as a fellow of the Institute of Legal Executives and then pass the LPC: approximately 17% of solicitors qualify this way.

Work

Most of the work of a solicitor involves giving legal advice to clients and carrying out administrative tasks, including conveyancing (dealing with the legal requirements of buying and selling property) and probate (drafting wills and acting as

---

Knowledge check 44

What are the qualifications needed to become a solicitor?

executors for the estates of deceased persons). Other routine work includes drawing up various kinds of contract, setting up companies and advising clients on family law problems.

Solicitors can act as advocates and represent clients in both Magistrates' and County Courts, in which they have 'rights of audience'. The opportunity to obtain rights of audience in the higher courts (Crown and High Court, and appellate courts) was first made possible by the **Courts and Legal Services Act 1990**, and was extended in the **Access to Justice Act 1999**. For rights of audience, solicitors have to qualify as solicitor-advocates.

Solicitors as a group actually do more advocacy work than barristers, since 97% of all criminal cases are tried in Magistrates' Courts, where both the prosecuting and the defending lawyer are solicitors. Even where a barrister has been instructed to represent the client in a court case, the solicitor still has an important role in the overall litigation process, handling various procedural aspects of the case such as evidence gathering and discovery of documents.

Solicitors usually work in partnerships. There has been a trend in recent years for firms of solicitors to merge into larger partnerships, which in turn has led to increasing specialisation.

Barristers

Qualifications

Barristers must be graduates, although their degree need not be in law (if it is not, they must take the GDL).

In order to continue their professional training, potential barristers must become a member of one of the four Inns of Court — Gray's Inn, Lincoln's Inn, Inner Temple or Middle Temple. The Inns are independent of one another and all have libraries, award scholarships and organise lectures and 'moots' (mock trials). Before being 'called to the Bar' by his or her Inn, the student must be accepted for and complete the Bar Professional Course (BPTC) which teaches the practical skills of advocacy and drafting pleadings and negotiation; the student must also have 'dined in' on 12 occasions (this rule now includes attending residential courses).

Having been called to the Bar on passing the BPTC, the student must obtain a 1-year pupillage at a set of chambers with an experienced barrister, who acts as a 'pupil master'. After the first 6 months of pupillage, barristers can appear in court in minor cases by themselves. A programme of continuing education is organised by the Bar Council during this period. To practise as an independent barrister (as a member of the Bar), the barrister finally has to secure a tenancy in a set of chambers.

Work

Barristers belong to a 'referral profession': this means that members of the public usually consult a solicitor first, who will then instruct a barrister if it is considered necessary. This process is similar to that of seeing a general practitioner first with a

Examiner tip

In a question on the work of a solicitor, include an explanation of the litigation role when working with a barrister.

Knowledge check 45

What are all the stages that must be followed in order to qualify as a barrister?

medical problem, and then being referred by the GP to a hospital consultant if the problem is serious. Barristers may, however, be engaged directly by certain professionals, such as accountants, and, since 1996, by members of the public whose cases have been handled by Citizens Advice Bureaux staff.

In 2004, the Bar Council permitted **Direct Public Access** (DPA), whereby for the first time any individual or company may go to a barrister directly for advice in civil law matters, provided the barrister has undertaken a qualifying course run by the College of Law. This change does not cover criminal, family or immigration work, so a large section of the Bar is not affected.

Examiner tip

In a question on the work of barristers, include a short paragraph on the 'cab-rank' rule.

Barristers are obliged under the **'cab-rank' rule** to accept any case referred to them, provided it lies within their legal expertise, the appropriate fee has been agreed and they are available at the time to accept the brief. This means that barristers cannot refuse to accept instructions in a case on the grounds of their own beliefs, the nature of the case or the character of the person on whose behalf they are instructed.

Most of the work of barristers involves advocacy in any court, as they have full rights of audience in all English courts. This work includes holding conferences with clients, presenting the case, cross-examining witnesses, summing up all the relevant case materials and arguing why the judge should decide in favour of the client.

The other main activity of barristers is that of providing counsel's opinions to solicitors on behalf of clients who require a specialised second opinion. Barristers may also negotiate settlements on behalf of clients, and offer mediation services to resolve the dispute between the parties.

Most barristers are self-employed and work from a set of chambers with other barristers, who share administrative and accommodation expenses. A clerk is employed, whose work involves booking cases and negotiating fees. However, approximately 20% are 'employed barristers' who work for an employer in industry, commerce or central or local government. This is known as the 'Employed Bar'.

Examiner tip

In a question on the work of barristers, include a short sentence on the work of QCs.

After 10 years in practice, barristers may apply to become a Queen's Counsel or QC, which is called 'taking silk' as they wear a court gown made of silk. Approximately 10% of barristers are QCs. Becoming a QC is a required step for most barristers if they aspire to be circuit or High Court judges. QCs are usually specialist barristers in a particular area of law and as such would undertake more challenging cases, especially appeals to the Court of Appeal and the Supreme Court.

In 2011, the successful 120 applicants included: 27 women (66% of those who applied); 12 ethnic-minority applicants (60% of those who applied); 2 solicitor-advocates and one employed barrister.

Legal executives

Qualifications

Most firms of solicitors employ legal executives, who do much of the basic work of solicitors — especially conveyancing and probate. Their qualifications are laid down by the Institute of Legal Executives (ILEX). To qualify as a legal executive, the minimum academic qualification is 4 GCSEs including English Language. During the period of work-based training in a solicitor's office, the trainee will have to pass the ILEX Professional Diploma in Law and Practice (Level 3).

The second stage of training to become a legal executive lawyer involves passing the ILEX Higher Diploma (Level 6) Course in Law and Practice which is usually studied part-time over 2 years.

It is then possible for an ILEX member to qualify as a solicitor by completing the 2 years' training contract, but if the legal executive has already qualified as an ILEX fellow (by working and training under the supervision of a solicitor for 2 years), he/she is exempt from having to undertake the training contract stage.

Work

A legal executive is a qualified lawyer specialising in a particular area of law. The role of legal executive lawyers is similar to that of a solicitor — they will have their own clients (with full conduct of cases) and they can even undertake representation in court where appropriate.

Depending upon which area of law they work in, legal executive lawyers may handle the legal aspects of a property transfer, be involved in actions in the High Court or County Courts, draft wills, draw up documents to assist in the formation of a company, or advise husbands and wives with matrimonial problems or clients accused of serious or petty crime.

Legal executive lawyers most often specialise in the following areas of law: civil litigation (such as personal injury; debt recovery; housing; employment); criminal litigation; family law and conveyancing. Legal executives may also work for a local authority or private company.

Examiner tip

In any question on becoming a solicitor, include a short paragraph on the 'legal executive route'.

Knowledge check 46

List three types of work that may be carried out by legal executives.

Solicitors

Qualifications:

- law degree (or non-law degree and GDL)
- Legal Practice Course (LPC) then 2-year traineeship
- entry onto the rolls of the Law Society
- ILEX route: pass the ILEX Professional Diploma in Law and Practice and the Higher Diploma. Then either qualify as an ILEX fellow or take the 2-year training contract

Work:

- non-litigious: giving general legal advice to clients, including conveyancing and probate, and setting up companies and advising on family law problems
- litigious: representing clients in Magistrates' and County Courts, or, if qualified as solicitor-advocates, in Crown Courts, the High Court and Appeal Courts. Solicitors also deal with all the procedural work involved in taking a case to court

Barristers

Qualifications:

- graduate entry only — law degree or non-law degree with GDL
- join an Inn of Court and pass the Bar Professional Course (BPTC)
- called to the Bar by Inn of Court
- obtain 1-year pupillage and then obtain a tenancy in a set of chambers

Work:

- referral profession unless client as Direct Public Access

Summary

Summary

- main work is to represent clients in court — barristers have full rights of audience in all English courts and tribunals
- barristers also provide 'counsel's opinion' to solicitors
- barristers must follow the 'cab-rank' rule
- they will also negotiate on behalf of clients and may provide a mediation service as an alternative to court action
- after 10 years in practice, barristers may apply to become QCs

Legal executives

Qualifications: during the period of work-based training in a solicitor's office, the trainee will have to pass the ILEX Professional Diploma and Higher Diplomas in Law and Practice

Work:

- specialist in an area of law, e.g. conveyancing and probate
- limited rights of audience in Magistrates' and County Courts

Funding of advice and representation

Society requires that all its members keep the law. It therefore follows that all citizens should not only be equally bound by the legal system but also be equally served by it. Yet almost a century ago, Lord Justice Mathew commented: 'In England, justice is open to all — like the Ritz Hotel.' In other words, anyone can go there, but only if they can afford it.

Since the end of the Second World War, the state has tried to provide a comprehensive system of free or subsidised legal advice and representation. However, since the 1990s, the bill for this system of legal aid has increased tremendously, from a figure of about £400 million to the present level of £2 billion. In the **Legal Aid, Sentencing and Punishment of Offenders Act 2012**, the coalition government is trying to cut £350 million from the legal aid budget by cutting provision for either advice or representation from such areas as debt, housing, employment, welfare benefits, education and clinical negligence. The financial limits of legal aid and advice schemes combined with the high fees charged by lawyers mean that large numbers of the population are unable to access legal advice. This is referred to as the 'unmet need for legal services': only the very rich, through paying privately, or the very poor, through legal aid, are capable of taking cases to court.

The **Access to Justice Act 1999** created the Legal Services Commission (LSC), an executive agency with overall responsibility for state funding of advice and representation. This replaced the Legal Aid Board. In contrast to the previous system, the commission has been given a fixed annual budget (currently around £2 billion per year) and allocates funding to the Criminal Defence Service (responsible for criminal matters) and the Community Legal Service (responsible for civil matters). The Criminal Defence Service (CDS) takes priority in the allocation of funding; it is a demand-led scheme and all eligible persons will be funded.

Under the 2012 Legal Aid Act the Legal Services Commission and the Criminal Defence Service are to be abolished and their responsibility for both civil and criminal legal aid transferred to the Director of Legal Aid Casework, who will be a senior civil servant in the Lord Chancellor's Department.

Sources of funding and legal advice

Solicitors

They are usually readily available in all towns and cities, and are able to offer professional legal advice to clients on a wide range of problems — criminal law, family law, wills and probate, civil claims, employment, consumer problems and property law and conveyancing. In more difficult cases, solicitors will recommend obtaining counsel's opinion from a specialist barrister. However, with increasing specialisation within larger solicitors' firms, many solicitors will no longer be able to offer advice across such a wide range of issues. They will of course charge fees which typically can be at the rate of £200–300 per hour. Many solicitors offer a free half-hour interview, and some will even offer their services 'pro bono' — free of charge in particular cases.

Citizens Advice Bureaux (CAB)

These are free of charge to the public and are funded by the Community Legal Service (CLS) and local authorities. Staff are generally not legally qualified. However, in matters such as housing, welfare benefits and debt counselling, they will have as much experience as many solicitors.

Law centres

There are only about 60 law centres in England and Wales and like CAB, they are funded by CLS and local authorities and the advice they provide is free. They employ qualified solicitors and barristers who will advise mainly on housing, employment, welfare and immigration problems. They will not deal with criminal law problems or conveyancing or probate.

Private legal insurance

Such policies provide legal advice and representation to policy holders, covering most types of legal problem which could result in litigation. Much more common are motor and house insurance policies which will provide legal advice and representation in the event of litigation arising from a road traffic accident or from an injury arising from a house accident, e.g. a falling tile which strikes a passerby. Such cover will be provided very cheaply as part of the policy.

Trade unions and professional bodies

Trade unions and professional bodies such as the British Medical Association (BMA) provide advice and legal representation in any dispute involving employment, e.g. unfair dismissal, discrimination cases, redundancy.

Other sources of legal advice

These include:
- independent advice centres — Age Concern, Shelter
- local authority services — Trading Standards, Environmental Health, housing advice centres, welfare rights units

Examiner tip
The key sources of legal advice, apart from private solicitors, are CAB and law centres.

Knowledge check 47

What are the advantages of going to a solicitor for legal advice?

- Race Equality Councils
- the Free Representation Unit in London, which handles 1,000 tribunal cases a year on a *pro bono* basis
- ALAS — the Law Society's free Accident Legal Advice Service, aimed at helping accident victims recover compensation
- internet advice websites

The civil scheme

The following schemes are run by the CLS:

- **Legal help** provides initial advice and assistance with any legal problem, but is subject to a tight means test. Help is available from a solicitor or other legal adviser who holds a contract with the Legal Services Commission. Under this scheme, legal advice up to a limit of £500 may be provided to the client.
- **Help at court** allows for a solicitor or legal adviser to speak on the client's behalf at certain court proceedings without formally acting for him or her in the whole proceedings, e.g. an application to suspend a warrant for possession in a housing case.
- **Approved family help** provides assistance in a family dispute, including facilitating a resolution through mediation.

Civil legal aid

The funding for civil legal aid is controlled by the CLS and covers all the work involved in bringing an action to court or defending an action in court, including representation. Since the **Access to Justice Act 1999**, all actions for recovery of money damages, especially personal injury cases, have been 'diverted' to conditional fee agreements — see below. Such legal aid funding as is still provided is targeted on child protection cases, cases involving breaches of human rights and social welfare cases, including housing and employment rights.

Eligibility for funding depends on a means test, which considers an applicant's disposable income and capital. Those whose income and capital are below the minimum limits will pay no contributions, but if income or capital is between the lower and upper limits, a contribution must be paid. There is also a merits test to ensure that such funding is only given where the case has a good prospect of success and where the award of damages will exceed the costs of the case.

Conditional fee agreements (CFAs)

Conditional fee agreements were first introduced into English law in 1995 under the **Courts and Legal Services Act 1990** (the implementation of the Act was delayed), which allowed a form of contingency fee. Under the CFA scheme, solicitors and barristers can agree to take no fee if they lose a case and are able, if they win, to raise their fee up to a maximum of double the usual rate. (However, under a voluntary Law Society agreement, this 'uplift' is limited to a maximum of 25% of damages recovered.)

In order to ensure money is available to pay the other side's legal costs if the case is lost, the Law Society has arranged an 'after-the-event' insurance scheme whereby, for a relatively small amount, the claimant's liability for such costs is covered.

Advantages of CFAs

- **No cost to the state.** The costs are entirely borne by the solicitor or the client, depending on the outcome of the case. Supporters of this scheme argue that, as well as saving public money, CFAs allow the government to fund properly those cases that still need state support and to direct more funds towards suppliers of free legal advice, such as the CAB.
- **Anyone can bring a case for damages.** One of the strongest arguments in favour of CFAs is that they allow cases to be brought by many people who would not have been eligible for legal aid or who could not reasonably have been expected to pay contributions under the existing civil legal aid scheme.
- **Wider coverage.** It looks likely that CFAs may be allowed for defamation actions and cases brought before tribunals — two major gaps in the existing legal aid scheme.
- **Discouragement of frivolous or weak cases.** In recent years, apparently trivial cases have been dragged through the courts at public expense, seemingly confirming the view that both solicitors and the Legal Services Commission are unable to apply the merits test sufficiently rigorously.

Disadvantages of CFAs

- **They are an inadequate substitute for legal aid in uncertain cases.** Most of those who have criticised CFAs accept that in uncertain cases they are a good *addition* to the state-funded legal aid system, but are concerned that they may not be adequate as a *substitute* for it.
- **Solicitors may only take on cases they are likely to win.** Critics, including the Bar, the Law Society and the Legal Action Group, have expressed strong concerns that certain types of case will lose out under the CFA scheme.
- **The insurance premiums to cover losing are high.** Most concern is expressed about medical negligence cases, which are generally difficult for claimants to win — the success rate is around 17%, compared to 85% for other personal injury actions.
- **There may be pressure to settle out of court.** The claimant may feel pressured by his or her lawyer to settle out of court (as this would guarantee the latter's uplift fee). If this happened, the claimant would potentially receive lower damages than if the case had been pursued in court.
- **There may be a conflict of interest between the solicitor and the client.** There is evidence in some cases that lawyers' advice about settlement may be influenced by their need to be paid rather than by the strict merits of any settlement offer.
- **There is public uncertainty as to what CFAs are and how the scheme operates.** In a research study entitled *Nothing To Lose* (reported in an article by Fiona Bawden, *New Law Journal*, 17 December 1999), the main finding was that clients think that CFAs are confusing.

Knowledge check 48

List the disadvantages of conditional fee agreements.

Criminal legal aid

Unlike legal aid in civil cases, state-funded criminal defence continues to be given on a demand-led basis. This means that, although the total legal aid budget is fixed, there is no set limit for criminal legal aid, and all cases that meet the merits and means tests are funded.

Under the **Access to Justice Act 1999**, the provision of funding is the responsibility of the Criminal Defence Service (CDS), which controls two schemes:

• The **duty solicitor scheme** was originally created under the **Police and Criminal Evidence Act (PACE) 1984** to provide a right to legal advice for suspects detained in police stations. It ensures access to a solicitor for advice and assistance is available 24 hours a day, free of charge and without means or merits tests. However, in practice cover can be described as 'patchy' with advice being given by telephone only, and often the advice will be provided by a legal executive or an inexperienced solicitor. At Magistrates' Courts, there is normally a duty solicitor available to give free advice on a defendant's first appearance if he or she does not have his or her own solicitor.
• The **criminal legal advice scheme** works in the same way as legal help (referred to on p. 73), with the same strict means test.

Criminal legal aid covers all types of criminal proceedings and pays for a solicitor to prepare the case and represent a client in court. It also covers the cost of a barrister, particularly if the case is heard in the Crown Court. The decision to grant aid depends on the two tests outlined below.

Merits test

The court decides whether it is in the interests of justice to grant legal aid. For serious cases, such as murder or rape, it will always be in the interests of justice to provide it. For less serious cases, such as minor motoring or non-imprisonable offences, the court is unlikely to agree to it. Between these extremes, the court decides on the basis of guidelines set out in the **Legal Aid Act 1988**.

'Interests of justice' criteria include cases where:
• the charge is so serious that, if convicted, the defendant risks the loss of liberty
• complex legal issues are involved
• the defendant is unable to understand the proceedings because of language problems etc.

Means test

The court looks into the applicant's financial position and the likely cost of the case:
• Applicants with the lowest means receive free legal aid, whatever the costs of the case.
• Applicants with more substantial means will not be granted legal aid if they can afford the likely costs.
• If the likely costs are large, applicants with reasonable means may be granted legal aid, but the court can require an applicant to pay a contribution towards the cost

of the case from both income and capital if he or she appears able to do so. Judges in the Crown Court are able to order convicted defendants to pay some or all of the cost of their representation.

Criticisms of legal aid

Legal help

This scheme was designed to bring in a new range of work, in part to address the issue of the unmet need for legal services for dealing with welfare and similar problems, which individuals have traditionally been reluctant to bring to lawyers.

Legal representation

The major problem is that for most money claims, civil legal aid is not available. There is greater emphasis on the use of conditional fee agreements. Under the **Legal Aid Act 2012** this problem will be exacerbated, as fewer people will qualify for civil legal aid. Where civil legal aid is available, it is still subject to severe means testing, and most people who are eligible are required to make a significant personal contribution.

Examiner tip

The key problem with civil legal aid is that money claims in most cases must be dealt with by CFAs.

The statutory charge

The assisted person in any proceedings funded by the Legal Services Commission applies this charge to money or property 'recovered or preserved'. The charge may result in the 'claw-back' of all the claimant's damages, which, as far as the client is concerned, may make the whole action a waste of time.

Recovery of costs

When a legally aided client loses a case, it is difficult, or often impossible, for the opponent to get costs back, as would normally happen in a civil case. This places the legally aided client at an unfair advantage.

Tribunals

Assistance for tribunal actions is only available in a very few cases (e.g. Prison Disciplinary Tribunals, Mental Health Tribunals).

Criminal legal aid

Research by McConville (1993) suggested that the standards of legally aided criminal defence work are low. Much of it is carried out by unqualified staff, there is little investigative work and solicitors push clients towards pleading guilty rather than taking time to prepare an effective defence. Since the merits test concentrates on the seriousness of the charge and possible penalty, it is more difficult for defendants to get legal aid for minor offences; sometimes it may be difficult to know whether the merits criteria apply until after a trial has started. Only about half of all defendants receive free legal aid at the Magistrates' Court, and about three out of four at the Crown Court.

Summary

Sources of funding and legal advice

In addition to obtaining advice and private representation from the legal profession, there are many other sources of both legal advice and representation:

- private legal insurance
- motor or house insurance policies
- 'law for free' work by lawyers
- Citizens Advice Bureaux (CAB)
- law centres
- trade union or professional associations
- state-funded legal aid

Comparison of advice obtained from solicitors and from other sources of legal advice:

- Solicitors are readily available.
- They offer advice across a wide range of legal problems.
- They can access counsel's opinions for more complex cases.
- They will charge fees.
- Legal advice from other sources will be more restricted.
- It may not be from a qualified lawyer.
- CAB and law centres do not charge for their advice.
- Advice obtained from insurance companies etc. is restricted to specific topics.

Civil legal aid schemes — run by the Community Legal Service set up under the **Access to Justice Act 1999**:

- Legal help provides initial advice and assistance with any legal problem, but is subject to a tight means test.

- Help at court allows for a solicitor to speak on the client's behalf at certain court proceedings without formally acting for him or her in the whole proceedings.
- Approved family help provides assistance in a family dispute.

Civil legal aid

- This covers all the work involved in bringing an action to court or defending an action in court, including representation. Eligibility for funding depends on a means test based on the applicant's disposable income and capital.
- Conditional fee agreements (CFAs) were introduced under the **Courts and Legal Services Act 1990**.
- Advantages of CFAs: no cost to the state and anyone can bring a case for damages
- Disadvantages of CFAs: inadequate substitute for legal aid in uncertain cases, and solicitors may only take on cases they are likely to win

Criminal legal aid

- The duty solicitor scheme provides a right to legal advice for suspects detained in police stations. At Magistrates' Courts, there is normally a duty solicitor available to give free advice on a defendant's first appearance.
- The criminal legal advice scheme works in the same way as legal help with the same strict means test.
- Merits test — interests of justice, e.g.:
  - the charge is so serious that, if convicted, the defendant risks the loss of liberty
  - complex legal issues are involved

The judiciary

In recent years, there have been significant changes to the qualifications and procedures for judicial appointment. The **Courts and Legal Services Act 1990** laid down the current statutory criteria for the appointment of each level of judge, but these were amended by the **Constitutional Reform Act 2005** and the **Tribunals, Courts and Enforcement Act 2007**. This Act also abandoned the old rule that judicial appointments should be based on rights of audience, thus accepting the criticism that there is no reason to assume that advocacy experience translates into judicial wisdom.

The statutory criteria are now:

- **district judge** — 5 years' qualification as a solicitor or barrister, 'gaining experience by being engaged in law-related activities'
- **Recorder (part-time judge)** — 7 years' qualification as a solicitor or barrister, 'gaining experience...'
- **circuit judge** — 7 years' qualification as a solicitor or barrister or sitting as a Recorder, or 3 years as a district judge
- **High Court judge** — 7 years' qualification as a solicitor or barrister, or 2 years as a circuit judge
- **Lord Justice of Appeal** — 7 years' qualification as a solicitor or barrister, but in practice, always appointed from High Court judges
- **Supreme Court Justice** — 15 years' qualification as a solicitor or barrister or at least 2 years holding high judicial office

Knowledge check 49

What Acts laid down the current eligibility criteria for judicial appointments?

Examiner tip

In any question on judicial appointments, you are required to know these different criteria.

Appointment procedures

The **Judicial Appointments Commission** (JAC) — created by the **Constitutional Reform Act 2005** — was set up in April 2006 and is responsible for the selection of all judicial office holders (all judges and tribunal members). It is the responsibility of the JAC to select candidates for judicial office on merit. It does this independently of government, through fair and open competition and by encouraging a wide range of applicants.

To become a deputy district judge or a district judge, suitably qualified candidates respond to advertisements placed in newspapers or professional journals or on the Lord Chancellor's Department (LCD) website and complete an application form. References are taken up and shortlisted candidates are invited to a 1-day selection procedure, during which they are interviewed and take various tests to measure legal and procedural knowledge. They also participate in mock trials. Successful candidates are nominated by the JAC to the Lord Chancellor for appointment.

For Recorders and circuit judges, the procedure is broadly the same, with advertisements placed by the JAC in the same media as mentioned above. Suitably qualified candidates apply by filling in an application form and providing a number of personal referees. After these references are taken up, candidates are shortlisted and interviewed by a panel of members from the JAC. Successful candidates are nominated to the Lord Chancellor, who formally makes the appointment.

Knowledge check 50

Briefly explain the process of appointing circuit court judges.

For appointment as a High Court judge, candidates are again required to apply to the JAC and provide references. Referees are interviewed by a panel chosen from the JAC, further references are taken up from the list of referees drawn up by the JAC and shortlisted candidates are interviewed by a panel chosen from the members of the JAC. The JAC then nominates one candidate to the Lord Chancellor for appointment. In the first 'batch' of High Court appointments, 144 candidates applied, 123 men and 21 women: 94 were barristers, 43 were circuit judges and seven were solicitors. Only three applicants were from ethnic minorities. The Lord Chancellor can accept the nomination, reject the nomination or ask the panel to reconsider the selection.

Appointments of Lord Justices of Appeal are similar to the procedure followed for High Court appointments, with the only significant difference being in the constitution of the panel that considers the applications. Under the **Constitutional Reform Act 2005 (CRA)**, this panel must contain:

- the Lord Chief Justice (LCJ) (or a nominee of the LCJ, who must be either a Head of Division or a Lord Justice of Appeal)
- a Head of Division or Lord Justice nominated by the LCJ
- the chairperson of the JAC
- a lay member of the commission

In practice, all appointments of Lord Justices of Appeal are made from the ranks of High Court judges.

Appointments to the Supreme Court are made under a different procedure because unlike all the other courts in which judges sit — County Court, Crown Court, High Court, Court of Appeal — the Supreme Court is a court of the UK, not merely of England and Wales. By convention, two members are from Scotland and one from Northern Ireland, and, although the CRA does not explicitly enact this convention, under s.27(8) 'the commission must ensure that between them the judges will have knowledge of, and experience in, the law of each part of the United Kingdom'.

No specific process is laid down in the statute, and therefore it is for the Commission to decide the nature of any competition for such an appointment. The Act does, however, require that part of the appointment procedure involve consulting:

- the Lord Chancellor
- the First Minister of Scotland
- the First Secretary of the Assembly of Wales
- the Secretary of State for Northern Ireland

The selection panel must comprise the president of the Supreme Court, the deputy president and one member each of the JAC for England and Wales, Scotland and Northern Ireland.

Knowledge check 51

Why is the procedure for appointing Supreme Court Justices different to other levels of judicial appointment?

Having received a nomination of one candidate, the Lord Chancellor has the same options open to him or her as for appointments to the post of High Court judge or Lord Justice of Appeal. However, Supreme Court appointments are recommended to the queen by the prime minister, and under s.26(3), the prime minister has to accept the name provided by the Lord Chancellor.

In 2011, Jonathan Sumption QC was appointed a Supreme Court Justice — the first appointment to this court directly from the Bar.

Criticisms of the appointment process

Despite the creation of the independent JAC, the majority of successful applicants to senior judicial appointments are white, male barristers. There has been no significant improvement in judicial diversity. In November 2011, there was still only one woman Supreme Court justice ((out of 12); four Lady Justices of Appeal (out of a total of 38 Court of Appeal judges), and only 16 women High Court judges out of 111. The lack of judges from ethnic minorities is an even greater challenge. This means that judges are as unrepresentative as ever.

Because of the high earnings made by successful QCs and senior solicitors, many of the best lawyers will not consider applying for a judicial post.

Finally, despite the additional training now given to judges, it is still possible for a judge to be appointed who will not be experienced or knowledgeable in the specific area of law which they will be involved in hearing. This can be a particular problem with Recorders whose main responsibility lies in trying criminal cases in Crown Courts but who may be civil law specialists; this same problem can also arise with High Court judges assigned to Queen's Bench Division.

Training

As all judges were formerly either barristers or solicitors, they are already highly skilled in legal knowledge and court procedure. This professional background has in the past led judges to believe that further training is unnecessary. However, nowadays, most full-time judges will have served as part-time judges, for example as Recorders or deputy High Court judges, before their full-time appointment. In addition, there is now a Judicial Work Shadowing Scheme which gives eligible legal practitioners who are considering a career in judicial office an insight into the work of a judge by spending up to 3 days observing the work of judges both in and out of court.

In the UK, judges still receive less training than in other countries, where there are 'career judges' — law graduates who decide to train as judges without first qualifying as lawyers. Trainee Recorders undertake a 4-day residential course before sitting in a Crown Court. The course includes lectures, sentencing and summing-up exercises, mock trials and equal treatment training. Before presiding over a Crown Court trial, Recorders in training sit alongside an experienced circuit judge.

In recent years, the Judicial Studies Board has received large increases in its operating budget and has arranged more training for judges and magistrates, including courses in ethnic awareness, human rights and computer use. The Civil Procedure Rules — reforms to the civil justice system — have prompted further judicial training. Judges certainly receive much more formal training than in the past. From April 2011, the responsibility of actually providing judicial training has been given to a new body, the Judicial College, whose activities fall under three main headings:

- initial training for new judicial office-holders and those who take on new responsibilities
- continuing professional education to develop the skills and knowledge of existing judicial office-holders
- delivering change and modernisation by identifying training needs and providing training programmes to support major changes to legislation and the administration of justice

A fundamental principle underlying the work of the Judicial College is that the training is for judges by judges.

Examiner tip
Exam questions often 'link' judicial appointment *and* training.

Functions

In civil courts, judges may be involved in allocating the particular case to the appropriate track, and also dealing with pre-trial issues such as discovery of documents and agreeing a timetable to be followed by the parties leading up to the

Knowledge check 52

What pre-trial work is performed by a judge?

Examiner tip

The pre-trial work of judges is often omitted from answers.

trial itself. At the trial, the judge will preside over the court, decide legal issues concerning admissibility of evidence and give a reasoned decision in favour of one of the parties. If the defendant is held liable, the judge decides the award of damages or other award such as an injunction. In appeal cases, judges have an important law-making role through the operation of the doctrine of precedent and statutory interpretation.

In criminal cases tried in Crown Courts, the judge may hold a pre-trial hearing to decide issues of bail and granting legal aid, and legal questions such as ruling on the admissibility of evidence. In the trial itself, the judge ensures that order is maintained, summarises evidence for the jury and directs it on relevant legal rules. If the defendant is convicted, the judge decides the sentence to be imposed.

- **District judges** work in County Courts, where they preside over small claims cases and have administrative responsibilities, and in Magistrates' Courts, where they sit by themselves.
- **Recorders** (part time) and **circuit judges** work in both Crown Courts and County Courts.
- **High Court judges** are assigned on appointment to a specific division of the High Court. Queen's Bench judges go on circuit to Crown Courts, where they try all Class 1 offences (such as murder) and most Class 2 offences (all other serious offences for which a life sentence could be imposed). They may also sit in the Court of Appeal (Criminal Division), together with a Lord Justice of Appeal, usually on appeals against sentencing rather than appeals against conviction.
- **Lords Justices of Appeal** sit in the Court of Appeal, either in the Civil or Criminal Division, usually in a panel of three.
- **Supreme Court Justices** sit in the Supreme Court, where they hear final appeals that must involve a point of law of 'general public importance'. Only about 70 cases are heard each year, the majority being tax cases. These judges also sit in the Judicial Committee of the Privy Council to hear cases from the few Commonwealth countries that allow such appeals to the UK, and from Scotland under the **Scotland (Devolution) Act 1998**.
- **Senior judges** are asked by government ministers to preside over judicial or public inquiries, e.g. the Dunblane Inquiry (Lord Cullen), the Hillsborough Football Disaster Inquiry (Mr Justice Taylor), the Arms-to-Iraq Inquiry (Lord Scott) and media phone-hacking (Lord Justice Leveson).

Examiner tip

When answering a question on the work of judges, ensure that there is no confusion between judges trying criminal and civil cases. This is a common problem.

Judicial independence

In the UK's legal system, great importance is attached to the idea that judges should be independent from any pressure from the government particularly, or from any political or other pressure groups, so that those who appear before them and the wider public can have confidence that their cases will be decided fairly and in accordance with the law. When carrying out their judicial function they must be free of any improper influence which could come from any number of sources, such as the government or the legislature, individual litigants, particular pressure groups, the media, self-interest or even other judges, in particular more senior judges.

Judicial independence is essential to the theory of the 'rule of law'. A. V. Dicey analysed this important concept in the nineteenth century and stated that 'no person is punishable except for a distinct breach of the law established in the courts', and not only is no one 'above the law, but...every man, whatever be his rank, is subject to the ordinary law of the realm'.

Separation of powers

This theory of judicial independence owes its origin to French philosopher Baron de Montesquieu with his theory of the 'separation of powers'. In this, he argued that the only way to safeguard individual liberties is to ensure that the power of the state is divided between three separate and independent arms: the legislature, the executive and the judiciary. Each arm should operate independently and be checked and balanced by the other two.

The separation of powers works in the following ways:

- **Tenure of office.** In England, all superior judges hold office 'during good behaviour', subject to removal only by the monarch by means of an address presented by both Houses of Parliament (**Act of Settlement 1701**). This has never happened to an English judge. Under the CRA 2005, the Office for Judicial Complaints (OJC) was appointed to investigate complaints made against judges.
- **Judicial immunity from suit.** No judge may be sued in respect of anything done while acting in his or her judicial capacity.
- **Immunity from parliamentary criticism.** No criticism of an individual judge may be made in either House except by way of a substantive motion. Political neutrality is also preserved in that judicial salaries are charged upon the consolidated fund, which removes the opportunity for an annual debate.

Note that full-time judges are excluded from membership of the House of Commons, and since the creation of the Supreme Court, its judges are no longer life-peers and cannot sit or vote in the House of Lords.

The value of judicial independence is highlighted by the increase in judicial review cases, in which judges are required to examine the legality or procedural correctness of government decisions. The responsibility of the judiciary to protect citizens against unlawful acts of government has thus increased, and with it the need for the judiciary to be independent of government.

There have been many instances where judges have overruled the decisions of government ministers, e.g. *A v Home Secretary* (2004) when the House of Lords ruled that control orders were unlawful. In recent years, there have been many judicial decisions concerning immigration appeals and appeals against deportation orders where home secretaries' decisions have been successfully challenged.

The independence of the judiciary is particularly necessary when judges have to chair inquiries into major cases and national events, e.g. the Hillsborough disaster, the Stephen Lawrence murder, the Arms-to-Iraq controversy and the Leveson Inquiry into the conduct of the press including allegations of phone-hacking.

A practical example of the importance of judicial independence is where a high-profile matter, which has generated a great deal of media interest, comes before the

Knowledge check 53

What are the three 'arms' of the state which need to be separate?

Knowledge check 54

What are the three ways in which judges can be shown to be independent?

Examiner tip

In a question on judicial independence, you should be able to explain a specific judicial review case in some detail to demonstrate a fuller understanding of why judicial independence is such an important concept.

court. Such matters range from the criminal trial of a person accused of a shocking murder to the divorce of celebrities and challenges to the legality of government policy, for example the availability of a new and expensive drug to NHS patients. In the 24-hour media age in which we live, it stands to reason that the judge hearing the case will often be under intense scrutiny, with decisions open to intense debate. It is right that this is so. But it is important that decisions in the courts are made in accordance with the law and are not influenced by such external factors.

Dismissal

All judges of the Supreme Court — of High Court rank and above — hold office 'during good behaviour' and may only be dismissed by the monarch following the passing of a substantive critical motion through both Houses of Parliament. The only occasion on which this procedure has been invoked was in 1830, when an Irish judge, Sir Jonah Barrington, was dismissed for embezzlement; it has never happened to an English judge.

It is possible for a judge to be removed on grounds of incapacity — through physical or mental ill-health — but this depends on the discretion of the Lord Chancellor. When Lord Chief Justice Lord Widgery became seriously ill towards the end of his judicial career, although suffering from a serious degenerative nervous disease he remained in his job.

Examiner tip
Ensure in questions on discipline/dismissal of judges that you can identify the difference between the procedures for inferior and superior judges.

The only example of a High Court judge effectively resigning is that of Mr Justice Harman, who left his position following serious criticism for taking more than 18 months to deliver a reserved judgement in the Court of Appeal.

Inferior judges such as circuit judges or District Court judges may be dismissed by the Lord Chief Justice acting together with the Lord Chancellor for misbehaviour, e.g. conviction for drink driving.

The **Office for Judicial Complaints** (OJC) was set up in April 2006 under the CRA 2005: 'The Lord Chancellor and the Lord Chief Justice have joint responsibility for a new system for considering and determining complaints about the personal conduct of all judicial office holders.' The OJC handles these complaints and provides assistance and advice to the Lord Chancellor and LCJ in the performance of their new joint role.

Complaints may be made to the OJC about the personal conduct of any judge, tribunal member or coroner. Examples of personal misconduct would be the use of insulting, racist or sexist language. The OJC cannot deal with any complaints about a judge's decision or about how he or she has handled a case — these matters are properly within the jurisdiction of the appeal process.

Knowledge check 55
What is the role of the OJC?

On completing its investigation of a complaint made against a judge, the OJC advises the Lord Chancellor and LCJ of its findings. They may then decide what action to take against the judge. They have the power to advise the judge as to his or her future conduct, to warn the judge, to reprimand, or even to dismiss an inferior judge. No disciplinary action may be taken against a judge unless both the Lord Chancellor and the LCJ agree the case merits it.

Appointment

The **Courts and Legal Services Act 1990** laid down the current statutory criteria for the appointment of each level of judge, but these were amended by the **Constitutional Reform Act 2005** and the **Tribunals, Courts and Enforcement Act 2007**. Levels of judge:

- district judge
- Recorder (part-time judge)
- circuit judge
- High Court judge
- Lord Justice of Appeal
- Supreme Court Justice

The Judicial Appointments Commission (JAC) is responsible for the selection of all judicial office holders.

Criticisms of the appointment process:

- Despite the JAC, most successful candidates are white, male barristers and in terms of the senior judicial appointments, there has been no significant change in judicial diversity.
- Because of high earnings made by successful QCs and by senior solicitors many of the best lawyers will not consider applying for a judicial post.
- It is still possible for judges to be appointed who will not be experienced or knowledgeable in the specific area of law which they will be involved in hearing.

Training

- All judges were formerly solicitors or barristers, and therefore have detailed legal knowledge and familiarity with court procedures. Most full-time judicial posts will be filled from part-time judges or from candidates who have been on the Judicial Work Shadowing Scheme.
- The Judicial Studies Board organises all judicial training. Responsibility for the actual training is given to the Judicial College whose responsibilities include initial training for new judicial office-holders and continuing professional education to develop the skills and knowledge of existing judges.

Functions

Civil courts:

- allocation of case to appropriate track and court
- pre-trial case management
- preside over trial
- decide outcome of case — if judgement in favour of claimant, decide award of damages or other remedy

Criminal courts:

- pre-trial hearing in Crown Court
- preside over trial and determine legal issues
- summarise the evidence for the jury and direct them on relevant legal rules
- if the jury returns guilty verdict, impose an sentence

Appeal Courts: important law-making role

Judicial independence

- Great importance is attached to the idea that judges should be independent from any pressure from the government, or from any political or other pressure groups.
- This is essential to the theory of the 'rule of law' and the separation of powers.

Dismissal

- All judges of the Supreme Court — of High Court rank and above — hold office 'during good behaviour' and may only be dismissed by the monarch following the passing of a substantive critical motion through both Houses of Parliament.
- Inferior judges may be dismissed by the LCJ acting together with the Lord Chancellor for misbehaviour.
- The Office for Judicial Complaints (OJC) handles complaints made against judges and provides assistance and advice to the Lord Chancellor and LCJ in the performance of their new joint role.

Questions & Answers

How to use this section

This section provides nine sample AS questions. Each question is followed by a brief analysis of what to watch out for when answering it (shown by the icon **e**). An A-grade answer is provided for each question. Examiner's comments (preceded by the icon **e**) show how marks are awarded.

The exam paper

The Unit 1 examination paper contains two sections: Section A — law making and Section B — the legal system.

Each section contains four three-part questions. Students are required to answer three questions — at least one each from Sections A and B:

- Part (a) of each question usually involves a straightforward description of the main facts of the topic (e.g. 'Describe how solicitors qualify and are trained').
- Part (b) is often an explanatory question on another issue within the topic (e.g. 'Explain how a claimant in a civil action may fund his or her claim').
- Part (c) requires analysis and evaluation (e.g. explain advantages and/or disadvantages).

Students should become familiar with the descriptors used by examiners in the award of marks for each paper:

- **Sound** — answer is generally accurate and contains material relevant to the potential content; support by references to relevant case examples and/or statutory authorities.
- **Clear** — answer is broadly accurate and relevant to the potential content, and is supported by some use of relevant case examples and/or statutory authorities.
- **Some** — answer shows some accuracy and some relevance to the potential content; few of the concepts of the potential content are established, as there are errors, omissions and/or confusion that undermine the essential features; occasional support by relevant case examples or statutory authorities.
- **Limited** — answer contains a few relevant facts with no additional explanation; no reference to case examples or statutory authorities.

Answers marked as mainly 'sound' will achieve a grade A, whereas answers that are mainly 'clear' will achieve a B or C. Answers that are 'some' will receive a D or E.

Effective answer planning

You are encouraged to spend time at the beginning of the examination planning your answers:

- First, read the question carefully. Are you required to outline, explain, discuss, analyse, compare or evaluate?

- Brainstorm the material you consider relevant to answer the different issues. Note down your ideas in the form of a spider diagram or under headings. This should help you to prioritise the points and indicate the links between them.
- Assess how much needs to be written on each component.
- Ensure your answer refers to case law and/or statutory authorities. Without such references, the answer will be graded as no more than 'some' or 'limited'.

Section A

Question 1 **Parliamentary law making**

(a) Briefly describe two influences on Parliament. (10 marks)

e The word 'briefly' indicates that neither should be described as fully as would be required if the question only asked about one.

(b) Describe the formal process used in creating a statute. (10 marks)

e 'Describe' requires you to write relevant facts about the formal process. To get higher marks your description needs to be full and developed with some detail.

(c) Discuss the advantages of this process. (10 marks)

e 'Discuss' requires you to identify advantages (at least three) but also to add evaluative comments.

A-grade answer

(a) The Law Commission was set up in 1965 to advise the government. It is a permanent, full-time body, headed by five Law Commissioners. The chairman is a High Court judge; the other four are members of the legal professions and academic lawyers. The Commission's work involves keeping all areas of law under review and producing a systematic programme of reform. The Lord Chancellor and other government departments may refer topics to it, or it may consider a topic of its choice after gaining government approval.

   The Commission researches an area of law and then produces a consultative paper setting out the present law, the problems with it and any proposals for change. Interested parties are able to put forward their views and a final report is published. This sets out any recommendations and a draft bill if legislation is proposed. The bill will only become law if Parliament decides to implement it. Legislation that has resulted from this process includes the Law Reform (Year and a Day Rule) Act 1996 and the Contract (Rights of Third Parties) Act 1999. There have been over 100 proposals put forward and about 70% have been adopted.

e Because the question asks for two influences, less is required for each than would be the case if only one were asked for. A 10-mark question just on the Law Commission would need more on the work done, e.g. in codifying law and repealing antiquated statutes, and more examples.

   A second area of influence is pressure groups, which are bodies of people with a shared interest in getting Parliament to change the law in certain areas. The groups may be ones with a cause, such as Shelter, Help the Aged, Friends of the Earth and Greenpeace, or groups with a sectional interest, such as the

Confederation of British Industry and trade unions, and cover many different areas of concern. They try to achieve their aims by targeting politicians, civil servants and local government offices. They lobby MPs, organise petitions and gain as much publicity for their cause as possible.

Some pressure groups only exist for a short time as they are set up to deal with a specific issue. Once that issue is resolved, they disband. An example is the Snowdrop Campaign, set up after the killing of the young schoolchildren in the Dunblane massacre in 1996. A successful campaign to ban the private ownership of handguns was launched.

Some pressure groups are more successful than others. Recent examples of successful campaigns are those of ASH to bring about a ban on smoking in public places and Stonewall to legalise gay marriage (achieved in the Civil Partnership Act 2004).

ⓔ **10/10 marks awarded.** This is a thorough and detailed response on pressure groups with good use of examples. As a whole the answer displays a clear understanding of both influences.

(b) The formal process of creating a statute always involves both the House of Commons and the House of Lords. Although important bills are nearly always introduced first in the Commons, bills can start their life in either House. Public bills are usually introduced by the government, and private members' bills are introduced by backbench MPs. The best-known example is the Abortion Act 1967. Public bills have general effect and are concerned with public policy that affects the law of the country.

ⓔ Notice that the answer goes straight to the formal process and does not spend time on drafting or Green and White Papers, which are not part of the formal process.

All public bills have to undergo a formal procedure in both Houses that can start in either House. At the first reading, which is purely formal, the title of the bill is read out. At the second reading stage, the bill is proposed by the government minister responsible and the House holds a full debate on the general principles of the bill. A vote to see if the bill should go further is taken at the end of the debate. The bill then passes to the committee stage, where the committee examines every clause in detail. Amendments can be made at this time. The report stage is when amendments are reported back to the whole House. There is then a third reading at which final amendments can be made.

The bill then passes to the other House (the House of Lords if it started in the House of Commons) and the same stages are repeated there. The difference is that in the House of Lords the whole House acts as a committee and all the amendments are debated and voted on. If disagreements between the Commons and Lords remain, these are usually resolved through negotiation or compromise, but ultimately the Commons has the power under the Parliament Acts 1911 and 1949 to ignore the objections of the Lords. This power is rarely used, but it was used to pass the Hunting Act 2004.

Once a bill has successfully passed through all the stages in both Houses it receives royal assent, after which it can become law. This royal assent is no longer given in person and the last time it was refused was in 1707. Without royal assent, the bill could not become law. At this point the bill becomes an Act of Parliament.

ⓔ 10/10 marks awarded. The student shows sound knowledge of the roles of both Houses of Parliament and the Crown in the creation of an Act of Parliament. The difference in the procedure at the committee stage in the House of Lords is mentioned and so are the powers under the Parliament Acts.

(c) One clear advantage of the process is that the MPs in the House of Commons are democratically elected and this gives legitimacy to the decisions that they make. Ordinary people have the opportunity to influence proposals by contacting their MP, and they have the ultimate power to vote the MP out at the next election. The prospect of defeat in a general election helps to ensure that governments take public opinion into account when they propose legislation.

Also the process is thorough and allows important bills that deal with major issues of economic and social policy to receive adequate debate and scrutiny, particularly in committee, before they become law. The many stages through which a bill has to pass should ensure that all aspects have been considered thoroughly.

Another advantage is that if all the parties agree that a new law is needed urgently, the process is sufficiently flexible to allow this to happen. For example, the Criminal Justice (Terrorism and Conspiracy) Act 1998 went through all its stages in 2 days, and the Northern Ireland Bill 1972 was passed in just 24 hours.

It could also be argued that it is an advantage that the House of Lords, although unelected, is a check on the executive's powers, acting as a safeguard to the abuse of power by a government which, because of its large majority, is able to force through almost any law it wants. The Lords has made the government rethink its proposals to abolish jury trials in fraud cases, for example. In January 2012 the Lords inflicted seven defeats on the Welfare Reform Bill and although these defeats were reversed in the Commons, the government has been forced to re-examine aspects of the bill and make changes in response to concerns raised by the Lords.

ⓔ 10/10 marks awarded. This answer identifies and discusses four relevant advantages. They are well explained and examples are included.

Question 2 **Delegated legislation**

(a) Outline two types of delegated legislation. (10 marks)

ⓔ The word 'outline' suggests fairly brief coverage of both types is required, but you must refer to examples.

(b) Explain how delegated legislation is controlled by the courts. (10 marks)

ⓔ Explaining is really the same as describing. Technical terms should be correct and examples provided.

(c) Discuss the disadvantages of delegated legislation. (10 marks)

ⓔ 'Discuss' requires you to identify disadvantages (at least three) but also to add evaluative comments.

A-grade answer

(a) Delegated legislation (secondary legislation) is legislation that is made not by Parliament but with its authority. Authority is given in an enabling Act, for example the Health and Safety at Work Act 1974 and the Court and Legal Services Act 1990.

ⓔ It is useful to briefly explain what delegated legislation is and the role of enabling Acts, but it is not absolutely necessary in this question. What is important when giving examples of any type of delegated legislation is to distinguish between the Act providing the authority and the piece of delegated legislation, as this answer does.

Statutory instruments take the form of rules, regulations and orders. Ministers and government departments are given the power to make statutory instruments relating to the jurisdiction of their ministry, for example the Minister of Transport has the power under various Road Traffic Acts to make detailed road traffic regulations. Under the Road Traffic Act 1998 the Traffic Signs Regulations 2002 were made which regulate the size and colour of road signs. Regulations are a good way of updating primary legislation and adapting the law to changing circumstances. For example, the Health and Safety at Work Act 1974 was updated through the Management of Health and Safety at Work Regulations 1992. Statutory instruments can also be used to implement EU directives, e.g. the Unfair Terms in Consumer Contracts Regulations, and Commencement Orders are used to bring Acts of Parliament into effect.

Bylaws are made by local authorities, such as county or district councils. They are local in effect, only applying in the area of the council concerned, and are involved with such things as parking restrictions and activities that can or cannot be carried out in certain public places, e.g. bylaws to ban the drinking of alcohol in parks. Under s.19 of the Public Libraries and Museums Act 1964 Cornwall County Council made bylaws about the use of libraries in the county. Public corporations and some companies can make bylaws to enforce rules covering behaviour in public places, e.g. the ban on smoking on the London Underground. Another example is that the National Trust can make bylaws affecting its properties. Also professional bodies like the Law Society or the Football Association can make regulations affecting their own members. All bylaws have to be approved by the relevant government minister.

ⓔ 10/10 marks awarded. The answer shows a clear understanding of statutory instruments and bylaws. Who makes each is explained and in both cases the answer outlines a variety of uses and refers to relevant examples.

(b) Delegated legislation can be challenged in the courts. Any person who has a personal interest in the delegated legislation (i.e. is affected by it) may apply to the court under the judicial review procedure. This is on the grounds that the delegated legislation is *ultra vires*, it goes beyond the powers granted by Parliament.

This can be in the form of either procedural *ultra vires*, where a public authority has not followed the proper procedure set out in the enabling Act (as in *Agricultural, Horticultural and Forestry Training Board* v *Aylesbury Mushrooms Ltd*, where the ministry failed to consult the interested parties) or substantive *ultra vires*, where the delegated legislation exceeds the powers in the enabling Act. In *R* v *Home Secretary ex parte Fire Brigades Union,* where the home secretary made changes to the Criminal Injuries Compensation Scheme, he was held to have exceeded the power given in the Criminal Justice Act 1988.

The courts might also decide that the delegated legislation is unreasonable as in *Strickland* v *Hayes*.

ⓔ 10/10 marks awarded. The grounds for judicial review are explained well, with both procedural and substantive *ultra vires* covered in detail. Relevant cases are given in support and this is a thorough description of judicial controls.

(c) There are a number of disadvantages of delegated legislation, the first of which is that it is undemocratic, because it is partly made by unelected people rather than by Parliament. Although it is true that most government ministers and all local authorities are elected, many of the bodies that make bylaws are unelected and also in practice the power to make statutory instruments is sub-delegated and made by civil servants in the relevant government departments rather than by the ministers who were originally given the delegated powers. Civil servants are unaccountable to the electorate.

Also there is little publicity compared to that received by Acts of Parliament, so people may be unaware that a particular piece of legislation exists. The sheer volume of delegated legislation is a further problem. There are in excess of 3,000 statutory instruments produced each year, some of which will set out new regulations affecting businesses and other organisations. Although all statutory instruments are published and available on the parliamentary website it is clearly difficult for those affected to keep track of the current law.

A further disadvantage is that controls are not always effective. Few statutory instruments have affirmative resolution, and MPs are too busy to look at those subject to negative resolution. Although there is a Scrutiny Committee which looks at all statutory instruments, it does not have the power to act independently and its recommendations are often ignored by Parliament as a whole. Control by the courts is dependent on someone challenging the validity of an instrument or bylaw under judicial review and these can only be on the basis that the body has exceeded its powers under the enabling Act.

Finally there have been concerns that sometimes the powers delegated are excessive. This is particularly the case with 'Henry VIII clauses', which allow delegated legislation to be used to amend or repeal Acts of Parliament. An example is the Hallmarking Act 1973.

ⓔ **10/10 marks awarded.** This answer considers four disadvantages, all of which are developed and discussed.

Question 3 Statutory interpretation

(a) Describe external aids.   (10 marks)

ⓔ A description of external aids requires reference to at least three, though only two need be in detail.

(b) Briefly describe two rules or approaches to statutory interpretation which can help judges to interpret statutes.   (10 marks)

ⓔ A brief description will be less detailed, but it must have case examples for both rules.

(c) Briefly describe the advantages and disadvantages of one of the rules of statutory interpretation.   (10 marks)

ⓔ Both advantages and disadvantages are needed. Include two of each with some evaluative comment.

> **A-grade answer**
>
> **(a)** External aids are things outside the Act. Dictionaries of various kinds are the most obvious external aid and they are used frequently as a means of discovering what words mean. For example in *Vaughan* v *Vaughan* (1973), where a man had been pestering his ex-wife, the Court of Appeal used a dictionary in order to define 'molest' and concluded that the definition was wide enough to cover his behaviour. In *Cheeseman* a dictionary was used to define the word 'passengers'.
>
> A second external aid is *Hansard*, the official report of what is said in Parliament. In *Davis* v *Johnson*, Lord Denning argued that not to refer to *Hansard* was like groping around in the dark without putting the light on. The House of Lords initially rejected Lord Denning's view, but it was eventually accepted by the Lords, subject to strict conditions, in *Pepper* v *Hart* (1993). Recent cases (for example *R* v *A*) have suggested that the courts may limit the use of *Pepper* v *Hart* to those cases against the government.
>
> When dealing with cases involving Acts that have introduced into English law an international convention or European directive, a wider use of *Hansard* is permitted (e.g. *Three Rivers DC* v *Bank of England*). Other external aids include previous Acts or cases and Law Reform reports from bodies such as the Law Commission. Also since 1999, all government bills are accompanied by explanatory notes, which provide guidance on complex parts of the bill.

ⓔ **10/10 marks awarded.** This is a strong answer. Notice that it focuses on two external aids, which are covered in detail and include case examples. Other external aids are referred to briefly.

> **(b)** The literal rule involves giving words their plain, ordinary, dictionary meaning. Lord Reid in *Pinner* v *Everett* referred to 'the natural and ordinary meaning of that word or phrase in its context'.

ⓔ When describing or explaining any rule, it is important to begin with a definition or a description of how the rule works, as this answer does.

The literal rule was used in *Whiteley v Chappell*. A statute made it an offence to 'impersonate any person entitled to vote' in an election. The defendant impersonated a dead person, and applying the literal rule, a dead person is not entitled to vote in an election. It was also used in *London and North Eastern Railway Co.* v *Berriman*, where Mrs Berriman was unable to obtain any compensation because her husband was killed while carrying out maintenance work (oiling points) on the railway line and not 'relaying or repairing' it. The Court decided that the literal meaning of relaying or repairing could not include maintaining.

e Case examples are also important when describing a rule. Three are given here and in two of them the answer explains how the case illustrates the rule.

The golden rule states that judges should use the literal rule unless it would produce an absurdity.

Under the narrow application, proposed by Lord Reid in *Jones* v *DPP*, if a word is ambiguous the judge may choose between possible meanings of the word in order to avoid an absurd outcome. For example, in *R v Allen* the Offences Against the Person Act 1861 made it an offence to 'marry' if you were already married. The court decided that 'marry' could have two meanings — to become legally married and to go through a ceremony of marriage. It would clearly be absurd to apply the first meaning, because no one could then be convicted of bigamy.

The wider application is where there is only one meaning but this would lead to an absurd or repugnant situation, and for policy reasons this would be unacceptable. An example is *Re Sigsworth*. Under the Administration of Estates Act 1925, the property of a person who died without making a will would pass to his or her next of kin. In this case, Sigsworth had murdered his mother, and it was clearly repugnant that a person who murdered his mother could then inherit her property.

e **10/10 marks awarded.** This answer explains the two rules clearly and gives examples to support the description.

(c) The mischief rule is regarded by most modern commentators as the best of the three rules, because it tries to give effect to the true intention of Parliament.

One advantage is that it allows judges, in Lord Denning's words, to 'fill in the gaps' when Parliament has left something out and to use common sense and change wording to reflect the problem that the Act was trying to deal with. *Smith v Hughes* could be seen as a sensible decision, reflecting what Parliament would have done had it been able to anticipate the situation. This leads to the additional benefit that Parliament does not have to spend time reviewing the Act and passing an amending Act to put right the issue identified by the court.

Another advantage is that it allows judges to interpret statutes in the light of changing social, economic and technological circumstances. A good example is the decision of the House of Lords in *Royal College of Nursing v DHSS*, which recognised that medical practice had changed since the passing of the Abortion Act because of the development of new techniques.

The most significant disadvantage is that the mischief rule also gives too much power to judges. It could be argued that it should be Parliament that makes any changes. It is not right that judges should try to second-guess what Parliament meant. Lord Denning's argument in *Magor and St Mellons* that judges should look for the intention of Parliament, even when there was no ambiguity, was criticised by Viscount Simonds as 'a naked usurpation of the legislative function under the thin disguise of interpretation'.

A further disadvantage of the mischief rule is that finding the intention of Parliament is not easy, even if *Hansard* is used; and by restricting the use of *Hansard* to statements by ministers, there is the danger that it will reveal the intention of the government but not necessarily the intention of Parliament.

e **10/10 marks awarded.** This response discusses both advantages and disadvantages of the mischief rule in detail. The comments are perceptive and supported by relevant authorities. Cases are used to back up the arguments, but time is not wasted outlining the facts.

Question 4 **Precedent**

(a) Outline two elements of precedent.   (10 marks)

(e) The command 'outline' requires brief coverage, but each element must be explained with some development.

(b) Briefly describe two ways in which judges can avoid precedent.   (10 marks)

(e) A brief description must still explain how each way avoids precedent and refer to examples.

(c) Discuss the disadvantages of precedent.   (10 marks)

(e) At least three disadvantages are required with evaluative comment.

A-grade answer

(a) The first element of precedent is *ratio decidendi* ('the reason for deciding'), which is the judge's written judgement setting out the facts and the legal principles used to reach the decision. The *ratio* forms the binding precedent to be followed in later cases. An example of *ratio decidendi* is the rule in *R* v *Nedrick* that if a jury considers that the defendant foresaw death or serious injury as a virtual certainty, oblique intention may be inferred. Another example is the judgement in *R* v *Cunningham* that to be reckless you have to know there is a risk of the unlawful consequence and decide to take the risk.

A second element is hierarchy. Without a hierarchy of courts it would be difficult for precedent to work. The highest court is the Supreme Court (SC). All the other courts in England have to follow its decisions, but the Practice Statement 1966 allows it to depart from its own previous decisions when it appears right to do so. For example, *Pepper* v *Hart* overruled the previous House of Lords ruling in *Davis* v *Johnson*.

The Court of Appeal (CA) is bound to follow the decisions of the SC. The Civil Division is also bound to follow its own previous decisions, unless the exceptions in *Young* v *Bristol Aeroplane Co.* apply. The Criminal Division is bound by its own previous decisions, unless liberty is at stake (*R* v *Spencer*) or to ensure justice (*R* v *Simpson*).

The High Court is bound by the SC and the CA. The Crown Court, County Court and Magistrates' Court are all bound by the decisions of the courts above them. They are not bound by their own previous decisions.

(e) **10/10 marks awarded.** The answer identifies two relevant elements: *ratio* and hierarchy. Both are described and their importance to precedent is also mentioned. As precedent is based on decided cases, the use of cases is essential in the answer.

(b) The courts may be able to distinguish the present case from that in which the precedent was set if the judge finds that the facts of the cases are sufficiently different. The Court of Appeal did this in *Boardman* v *Sanderson,* where it was able to depart from the decision in *King* v *Phillips*. Another example is *R* v *Wilson*, which was distinguished from *R* v *Brown* and others. In *Brown* the defence of consent was not allowed as sadomasochistic acts did not qualify as surgery or tattooing, but in *Wilson*, where a man carved his initials into his wife's buttocks with a hot knife, the court distinguished *Brown* and said that this did amount to tattooing.

The second way in which a precedent can be avoided is through overruling. Judges in the higher courts can overrule the decisions of the lower courts if they decide that the legal principles are wrong. The 1966 Practice Statement in the House of Lords allowed the court to depart from its own previous decisions where it is right to do so. *R v Shivpuri* was the first criminal case in which the power under the Practice Statement was used. The House of Lords overruled its decision in *Anderton v Ryan* made just a few months earlier. The Supreme Court replaced the House of Lords in 2009 and has the same power to avoid precedent.

The Court of Appeal (Criminal Division) can overrule earlier Court of Appeal decisions in the interests of justice (*R v Simpson*). The Civil Division is more restricted and can only overrule earlier Court of Appeal decisions if one of the three situations outlined in *Young v Bristol Aeroplane Co. Ltd* applies.

@ **10/10 marks awarded.** This is another answer where the use of cases is important to illustrate how the methods work and several are used here. This answer deals thoroughly with two relevant ways in which precedents can be avoided.

(c) One disadvantage of precedent is the sheer volume of reported cases which makes it difficult to know all the cases that might be relevant, although this is less of an issue now that so many important cases are reported online. What does remain a problem is that there is difficulty in determining the *ratio decidendi* of some reported cases because of the way in which the judgement is written and also the fact that cases may have multiple ratios (as for example *Rylands v Fletcher*).

Another disadvantage is that the strict hierarchy means that bad or inappropriate decisions cannot be changed unless they are heard in a higher court that can overrule them. If the precedent is in the Court of Appeal as many are, a future case (because of the rule in *Young v Bristol Aeroplane Co. Ltd*) would have to be appealed to the Supreme Court in order to overturn it. This could only happen if it raised a point of law of public importance and if a potential appellant could afford to pursue the appeal.

A contrasting disadvantage is that the use of distinguishing has led to many precedents being avoided on the basis of what might appear to be only minute and illogical differences between some cases. Too many distinctions of this type can lead to unpredictability and uncertainty. An example is the case of *Wilson*, which was distinguished from *Brown* and arguably left greater uncertainty about the circumstances in which consent might be available as a defence.

Finally there is the issue that case law applies retrospectively. This could lead to unfairness and is what happened in *R v R*. The effect of this case was to turn an act that was lawful at the time it was committed into a serious criminal offence.

@ **10/10 marks awarded.** This response identifies several disadvantages, but they are all developed and commented on and in each paragraph a relevant case is referred to. It is clear that the student understands the significance of each disadvantage and is a reminder that you need to understand as well as memorise evaluative points that you make. Examiners can usually spot if a student has memorised something without actually understanding it.

Section B

Question 1 **Juries**

(a) Describe the selection of juries for Crown Court trials.   (10 marks)

ⓔ The command word 'describe' like 'explain' requires a fuller answer than 'outline' with statutory authorities used effectively.

(b) Explain the function of a jury in criminal trials.   (10 marks)

ⓔ Explaining is really the same as describing.

(c) Discuss the disadvantages of the use of juries in criminal cases.   (10 marks)

ⓔ 'Discuss' requires you to identify disadvantages (at least three) and to add evaluative comments.

A-grade answer

(a) The criteria for the selection of juries are laid down in the Juries Act 1974 as amended by the Criminal Justice Act 1988, which requires jurors to be aged 18–70, to be on the electoral register and to have been resident in the UK for 5 years from the age of 13. Jurors are summoned by random sampling carried out initially by the Central Jury Summoning Bureau. From the number summoned for jury service, after excusal or deferral the clerk will randomly select 20 as 'jurors in waiting', then the final 12 jurors are chosen.

ⓔ The first paragraph comprehensively covers the primary qualifications laid down in the relevant statute, before explaining how juries are actually chosen.

There are, however, certain people who are either disqualified from, or ineligible for, jury service. Those with a serious criminal record who have served a prison sentence within the previous 10 years or who have served any community sentence within the previous 5 years are disqualified. Under the Criminal Justice Act 2003, only the mentally ill are ineligible. Judges, lawyers and police officers are now eligible for jury service. Only those over 65 may be excused from jury service as of right. Some people may be excused at the discretion of the court, e.g. nursing mothers, students sitting public exams or those with a poor command of English, but most are now likely to have jury service deferred until a later date.

ⓔ This paragraph continues by explaining the issues of disqualification and ineligibility and the important changes made in the 2003 Act. Good examples are provided of excusal at the court's discretion.

Jurors may be vetted and challenged. Peremptory challenge by the defence (i.e. challenging without cause) was ended by the Criminal Justice Act 1988. Defence may now only challenge a juror with cause. The prosecution may require a juror to 'Stand by for the Crown', but this is rarely employed and it is usual for a reason to be given. More detailed checks on a juror's background may only be carried out with the approval of the Attorney General, and this will be given only in security or terrorist trials.

ⓔ **10/10 marks awarded.** The mark scheme for this question includes the topic of vetting and challenge, and this section ensures that the answer is 'sound'.

(b) The function of a jury in a criminal trial in Crown Courts is to decide the issue of guilt or innocence of the defendant. The jury acts as 'master of the facts', whereas the judge is 'master of the law'. The jury hears all the evidence in the trial, provided by both the prosecution and the defence. Jurors are encouraged to take notes and may ask questions of any witness through the judge.

ⓔ This is another straightforward and direct introductory paragraph which makes short, key points.

At the end of the trial, after closing speeches by counsel, the judge sums up the evidence and directs the jury on all relevant points of law. In a complicated trial, the judge may provide the jury with a series of questions to assist its deliberations. The jurors retire to a room where, in strict privacy, they consider their verdict. A foreman is selected to speak for the jury and should lead the jurors in their discussions.

ⓔ This paragraph amplifies the basic points by explaining *how* juries perform their function.

If after 2 hours 10 minutes the jurors have not reached a unanimous verdict, the judge may recall them to advise that a majority verdict upon which at least ten are agreed will be accepted — this was first provided by the Criminal Justice Act 1967. Only about one fifth of all verdicts are by a majority.

ⓔ This section on majority verdicts clearly establishes this as a 'sound' answer.

When a verdict has been decided, the jury returns to court and the foreman delivers the verdict to the judge.

ⓔ **10/10 marks awarded.**

(c) One of the most serious criticisms concerning juries is the high acquittal rate when compared to trials in Magistrates' Courts. However, such a comparison is not helpful, since the nature of summary cases is usually much more 'fact-based' and the great majority of defendants plead guilty. One factor leading to higher acquittal rates has been said to be the large number of middle-class, professional people who are able to evade jury service through ineligibility or excusal. One of the key sections in the Criminal Justice Act 2003 was the elimination of such categories, and this has led to more representative juries.

e This is a strong opening paragraph which addresses one of the most serious criticisms of juries and makes a good evaluative point about the change introduced in the CJA 2003.

> Particular concern is often expressed about the competence of juries to understand even 'basic' legal concepts such as 'reasonable doubt' and 'intent' and some weight was given to these concerns by the results of the New Zealand Law Commission research into juries.
>
> A further criticism is that jury trials are much more expensive than summary trials, but this criticism is misplaced. The major costs of Crown Court trials are those of professional judges, lawyers, expert witnesses etc. The average jury cost does not exceed £1,000.

e Recognise the significance of the point raised about why jury *trials* — and not juries — are so much more expensive than Magistrates' Court trials.

> The argument that juries have insufficient competence to deal with fraud cases was undermined by the research into the Jubilee Line case, which confirmed that the jury in that case fully understood the complex issues.
>
> Finally, there remains the serious issue of 'jury nobbling', whereby jurors are intimidated or bribed to acquit defendants. In order to protect jurors, the Metropolitan Police Force spends up to £4.5 million per year. Additional protection against nobbling was also introduced in the Criminal Procedure and Investigation Act 1996, which allows the retrial of a defendant acquitted as a result of jury nobbling. While this is a major problem, it cannot by itself even begin to justify the removal of juries from serious criminal trials in the UK.

e **10/10 marks awarded.** This is a 'sound' answer overall which covers all the key points in the potential content.

Question 2 Magistrates

(a) Describe how magistrates are appointed. (10 marks)

ℯ The command word 'describe' like 'explain' requires a fuller answer than 'outline' with statutory authorities used effectively.

(b) Explain the criminal jurisdiction of magistrates within the English legal system. (10 marks)

ℯ 'Explain' requires a fuller answer than 'outline' with statutory or case authorities used effectively.

(c) Briefly consider the advantages and disadvantages of magistrates within the English legal system. (10 marks)

ℯ A brief 'consideration' should explain two advantages and two disadvantages and include some evaluation.

A-grade answer

(a) In order to become a magistrate, a person can either apply to the local advisory committee or be nominated by local political parties or voluntary bodies. The statutory qualifications are that the applicant must be under the age of 65 and live or work within a short distance of the court within which he or she will normally be working. Although until recently applicants had to be 27 years old to be appointed, this is no longer a requirement, and some candidates as young as 19 have been appointed. Candidates are required to spend an average of half a day per week sitting in court. The current procedures for selection and appointment are contained within the Justices of the Peace Act 1979.

ℯ This is a strong opening paragraph which sums up the statutory qualifications.

Categories of people who are excluded from appointment include police officers, members of the armed forces, undischarged bankrupts and those who have a serious criminal record.

After application or nomination, references are checked, as is the person's criminal record. A shortlist is drawn up by the committee and two interviews are held: the first measures the candidate's general character; the second, which comprises a number of judging and sentencing exercises, assesses the candidate's judgement. After all the candidates have been interviewed, the committee meets to consider the various issues of balance. The Lord Chancellor has made it clear that he requires broadly equal numbers of men and women, and a wide spread of occupation, ethnic origin and, to a lesser extent, political affiliation and age. The committee will finally recommend names to the Lord Chancellor, who usually accepts these recommendations and will formally appoint the magistrates. At the conclusion of the selection and appointment procedure, successful candidates are formally sworn in as magistrates at a ceremony conducted by a senior circuit judge.

Before sitting in court, newly appointed magistrates are required to attend an extensive training and mentoring programme organised by the Judicial Studies Board — the Magistrates New Training Initiative 2.

ⓔ **10/10 marks awarded.** This is a very full answer which covers all the different stages of the appointment of magistrates, starting with the application/nomination stage, then explaining the statutory requirements, and stating those who are disqualified (often omitted) before describing the actual selection process. Although not specified in the question, it is always a good idea to mention the training given to magistrates.

(b) Magistrates play by far the largest role in the criminal justice system as they try about 97% of all criminal trials — all summary offences and most either-way offences. For either-way offences, there will be a preliminary hearing called 'plea before venue', where the accused person is given the choice of summary trial by magistrates or trial before judge and jury in the Crown Court. Offenders charged with indictable offences will be transferred to the Crown Court after the preliminary hearing under the Crime and Disorder Act 1998.

ⓔ This is a straightforward and direct introduction which deals effectively with the three different types of criminal offence.

Sentencing powers of magistrates in adult courts are a maximum fine of £5,000 and/or a prison sentence of 6 months.

Magistrates also try most offences committed by young offenders (aged 10–17), in the youth court. The only offence that cannot be tried here is murder. The youth court is less formal than the adult court and magistrates must have received additional training to carry out this work. The maximum sentence available in this court is a 2-year training and detention order.

Other functions within the criminal justice system include bail applications (under the Bail Act 1976), applications for legal aid, and the issue of search and arrest warrants.

Finally, lay magistrates continue to sit with a circuit judge in appeals to the Crown Court against conviction.

ⓔ **10/10 marks awarded.** This is a strong answer, although brief. It deals with the sentencing powers before covering the work of the youth court — which is all too often omitted by students — and magistrates' work in dealing with bail, legal aid and warrants. Finally, there is a mention of the work that magistrates carry out together with a circuit judge in the Crown Court sitting in an appellate capacity — also often omitted.

(c) Magistrates have historically been an important part of the criminal justice system, and they enable members of the community to become involved in the administration of criminal justice. They are the most representative type of judges — unlike our professional judiciary, almost 50% are women with almost 8.5% drawn from ethnic minorities. They also provide 'local' justice, as they have to live within a short distance of their bench; this gives them a greater awareness of local events and local patterns of crime.

Because magistrates are unpaid, Magistrates' Courts are the only 'profit-making' component of the criminal justice system, as the value of fines exceeds the overall costs of these courts. They are also much quicker in bringing cases to trial than is the case with Crown Courts, where delays of up to a year are not uncommon. This was a particular feature following the serious riots in London and other cities in 2011. Another advantage is that they sit in panels of three — effectively a 'mini-jury'.

ⓔ The advantages are clearly explained and a good illustrative point is made about how representative magistrates are.

The most significant disadvantage of magistrates is the serious level of inconsistency in their sentencing. Surveys continue to show that some benches are ten times more likely to impose custodial sentences than neighbouring benches. This is clearly unfair — simple justice demands that similar offenders receive broadly similar sentences. It has been argued that as more new summary offences are being created together with different forms of sentencing, the work of magistrates is now much more complex. However, they also receive much more training and there is a qualified legal adviser in court to advise them on legal issues.

It is also argued that because magistrates are not legally qualified, this justice is 'amateur justice'. This fails to take into consideration the fact that magistrates are now selected far more carefully and receive much more detailed training under the Magistrates National Training Initiative (MNTI 2) than was the case several years ago. Furthermore, the importance of the partnership that magistrates form with a legally qualified clerk needs to be noted. The overall success of Magistrates' Courts is, however, confirmed by the low 'success' rate of appeals against both sentence and conviction.

ⓔ **10/10 marks awarded.** This is a very full answer with a sound balance of material for both advantages and disadvantages. Note that for each point, there is a brief explanation — far removed from bullet-point answers. The reference to the London riots is both topical and useful, as is the fact that on the disadvantages, the answer explores how relevant these are.

Question 3 Legal professions

(a) Outline the qualifications and training required to become a solicitor.   (10 marks)

ⓔ The command 'outline' requires a brief factual account only.

(b) Briefly describe the work carried out by both solicitors and barristers.   (10 marks)

ⓔ Since the work of both solicitors and barristers is included, only a brief factual account of each is required.

(c) Legal advice can be obtained by the public from solicitors and from other sources, such as Citizens Advice Bureaux etc. Briefly discuss the advantages and disadvantages of obtaining legal advice from solicitors and from other sources.   (10 marks)

ⓔ As both advantages and disadvantages are included, a 'brief description' need only cover two of each with little evaluative content.

A-grade answer

(a) In order to become a solicitor, most people take a university degree, not necessarily in law. If another degree is taken, or a non-qualifying law degree, a further year's study is taken to pass the Graduate Diploma in Law (GDL). The next part of the qualifying course is the Legal Practice Course (LPC), which is a 1-year, full-time course. Finally, students have to obtain a training contract in a solicitors' firm, which lasts 2 years.

After the successful completion of the traineeship, the trainee will be admitted as a solicitor by the Law Society and his or her name will be added to the roll of solicitors. It is also possible for mature entrants to qualify as solicitors by first qualifying as legal executives and then as Fellows of ILEX, after which they take the LPC or the 2-year traineeship. Even after qualification, solicitors are required to attend specialised training courses as part of their continuing professional development.

ⓔ **10/10 marks awarded.** Although this is a short answer, it deals with every aspect of the question, both qualifications and training. Students should note how well structured this answer is. It is always recommended that such answers include a reference to the ILEX route of qualifying as a solicitor.

(b) The work of solicitors is largely non-litigious, although they do have rights of audience in both County and Magistrates' Courts. Their work involves conveyancing (transferring property rights) and probate (wills and executory work), together with giving general legal advice to clients, which could include family law, employment law or setting up companies etc. Under the Courts and Legal Services Act 1990 (as amended by the Access to Justice Act 1999), solicitors can acquire higher-court rights of audience by qualifying as solicitor-advocates.

Most solicitors work within a partnership with other solicitors. Over recent years, in both London and large cities, there has been a trend for law firms to merge to create much larger partnerships, which in turn has led to greater specialisation in the work undertaken by solicitors.

ⓔ Note the use of statutory authorities which is always necessary for an answer to be graded 'clear' or 'sound'.

The Bar is a referral profession, i.e. clients have to see a solicitor first (unless they are members of another profession, e.g. accountants, in which case there is direct professional access), although Direct Public Access is now available for certain kinds of case. Barristers are self-employed and usually work from a set of chambers where they share administrative and secretarial expenses with other barristers. The majority of barristers concentrate on advocacy, representing clients in court, but they also provide specialist advice through counsel's opinions to solicitors. The litigation work of a barrister also includes drafting pleadings prior to the case coming to court. Barristers have rights of audience in all English courts.

ⓔ 10/10 marks awarded. This is a well-balanced answer in which the functions of each professional are described fully and clearly. Use of specialised legal language is accurate and there is appropriate statutory reference. The work of solicitors is explained well — usually, students fail to distinguish between the non-litigious work and the court work undertaken by solicitors. The key strength of this essay lies in its balanced plan; its structure addresses all the issues raised in the question.

(c) Solicitors are usually readily available in all towns and cities, and are able to offer professional legal advice to clients on a wide range of problems — criminal law, family law, wills and probate, civil claims, employment, consumer problems and property law and conveyancing. In more difficult cases, solicitors will recommend obtaining counsel's opinion from a specialist barrister. However, it is also true that with increasing specialisation within larger solicitors' firms, many solicitors will no longer be able to offer advice across such a wide range of issues. Obtaining such advice will also be much more expensive than from a Citizens Advice office or law centre which will be free, unless the solicitor is able to offer to work on a 'pro bono' basis. Many solicitors are, however, prepared to offer up to 1 hour's interview with potential clients free of charge. If the legal problem is a complex one, solicitors will be able to seek more specialised advice from a barrister. The solicitor will also be able to take the case to court and represent the client.

ⓔ This is a sound explanation of the advantages and disadvantages of obtaining advice from solicitors.

The great advantage of Citizens Advice Bureaux (CAB) and law centres is that the advice will be free. CAB also handle a wide range of legal problems — benefit entitlement, employment issues, family law, education law, consumer affairs, immigration and discrimination. Their volunteer staff, however, will not usually be legally qualified so may not be able to deal with more complex problems. Law centres do employ qualified barristers and solicitors but there are far fewer such centres as central and local government funding for these has been reduced in recent years. As for other sources of legal advice such as membership of trade unions or professional organisations or from motor insurers etc. such advice is restricted to specific legal issues — trade unions will only advise on employment law issues, motor insurers will provide legal advice and representation for a criminal prosecution following a road traffic accident.

@ **10/10 marks awarded.** This is another sound answer — it is strengthened by the inclusion of law centres, trade union membership and motor insurance policies.

Question 4 Judges

(a) Explain the process of judicial selection and appointment. (10 marks)

ⓔ 'Explain' requires a full and developed factual account with effective use of case/statutory authorities.

(b) Briefly explain the functions of judges in our legal system. (10 marks)

ⓔ Less detail is required here, but your answer still needs to include the work of judges in civil and criminal trials, as well as the work of appellate judges.

(c) Discuss the importance of judicial independence. (10 marks)

ⓔ 'Discuss' requires the answer to explain *all* the key elements of judicial independence together with some evaluative comment. Some case example(s) are necessary.

A-grade answer

(a) The criteria for judicial appointment were laid down in the Courts and Legal Services Act 1990, but these were amended by the Tribunals, Courts and Enforcement Act 2007. They are different for different types of judge, for example to become a circuit judge, a candidate must have been a solicitor or barrister for 7 years or have been a Recorder; a High Court judge requires to have been a solicitor or barrister also for 7 years or have been circuit judge for 2 years.

ⓔ This is an effective opening paragraph covering statutory authorities and providing two examples of criteria for judicial appointment.

New procedures for judicial appointment were laid down in the Constitutional Reform Act 2005, which established the Judicial Appointments Commission (JAC).

The selection and appointment procedure for district judges, Recorders and circuit judges is broadly the same. Suitably qualified candidates apply to the JAC in response to advertisements. References are checked and shortlisted candidates are interviewed by a panel selected from the JAC. The JAC then recommends suitable candidates to the Lord Chancellor for appointment.

To become a High Court judge, candidates again must apply to the JAC — references are checked and shortlisted candidates and some of their referees are interviewed by a panel of members of the JAC. Again, successful candidates are recommended to the Lord Chancellor for appointment.

Lord Justices of Appeal are always appointed from the ranks of High Court judges and again the procedure involves application to the JAC. Applicants are interviewed by a panel comprising the Lord Chief Justice and a Head of Division, and the chairperson of the JAC plus a lay member.

Supreme Court justices are drawn mainly from Lord Justices but, since the Supreme Court is the supreme UK Court of Appeal, senior Scottish and Northern

Irish judges are also appointed. The Lord Chancellor provides one name to the prime minister for recommendation to the queen. This nomination may not be rejected by the prime minister.

ⓔ **10/10 marks awarded.** It is always recommended that in such questions, students begin by referring to the statutory qualifications with one or two examples, then describing the appointment procedure for each level. Often students make the serious mistake of 'lumping' all the judges together. The role of the JAC is well described. The description of Supreme Court appointments (not often described) confirms this as a 'sound' answer.

(b) The functions performed by judges depend on the court in which they sit. In civil cases, they will hold pre-trial hearings to set a timetable for the trial; they then preside over the trial, hear all the evidence led by both sides and then make a decision, which has to be presented to the parties in detail. If the judge holds the defendant liable, damages will then be determined. In addition, the High Court has the jurisdiction of conducting judicial reviews, which have grown in number considerably in recent years. This requires judges to assess the legality or reasonableness of decisions or actions of public bodies, especially those of government ministers.

ⓔ This is a sound opening paragraph dealing with the functions of judges in civil cases in a simple, straightforward way. The mention of judicial review ensures this is a sound response.

In a criminal trial in the Crown Court, the judge will also deal with pre-trial hearings to deal with bail and other legal points. During the trial the judge has to keep order, decide legal questions such as the admissibility of evidence, direct the jury on the law and sum up the evidence impartially. If the jury finds the defendant guilty, it is then the judge's duty to pronounce sentence.

ⓔ This short paragraph on criminal trial functions 'mirrors' the opening paragraph on civil trial functions.

In both the Court of Appeal and the House of Lords, judges have an important law-making role, through both the doctrine of judicial precedent and statutory interpretation. Cases such as *Attorney General of Jersey* v *Holley*, which changed the law of provocation, or *Hedley Byrne* v *Heller* on recovery of pure economic loss, are good examples of law changes. Such senior judges are also often asked by the government to hold judicial inquiries, e.g. the Leveson Inquiry into press phone hacking.

ⓔ **10/10 marks awarded.** This answer fully addresses each element of the question and is clearly structured, covering civil matters first then criminal ones, before dealing with judges sitting in an appellate capacity. Good examples are also provided.

(c) In our legal system, great importance is attached to the idea that judges must be independent from any pressure from the government or any other body. This ensures that they can try cases impartially. Under Article 6 of the European

Convention on Human Rights, incorporated into UK law by the Human Rights Act 1998, every citizen has the right to be tried by a 'fair and independent tribunal'. Judicial independence is also essential to the theory of the rule of law which states that 'no man is above the law' but subject to the same legal process as anyone else. This is especially important in judicial review cases where citizens argue that government ministers have exceeded their legal powers or have acted unreasonably. A good example of this is *A v Home Office* where the House of Lords ruled that the government had breached individuals' rights by detaining them without limit of time and with no charges against them under anti-terrorist laws.

ⓔ This is a strong introductory paragraph which clearly explains the meaning of judicial independence, and then continues by showing its importance. The 'rule of law' argument is clearly presented. The case example greatly strengthens this answer.

A further measure of the importance of judicial independence is that it reflects the separation of government powers — the executive arm (the government), the legislative arm (Parliament) and the judicial arm (the judges). This theory which is the basis of good government ensures that there are checks and balances of the power of each part of government. Finally, the independence of judges from the government allows judges to preside over major inquiries following disasters or other issues of great public importance such as the Leveson Inquiry into media phone hacking.

ⓔ While brief, this account of the separation of powers theory is clearly outlined. The example of the Leveson Inquiry lends weight to the argument.

Judicial independence is guaranteed by the fact that superior judges hold office during good behaviour and can only be dismissed following an address to the queen moved in both Houses of Parliament. They are also immune from any legal action arising out of a decision they make in their judicial capacity, and they cannot be criticised personally in Parliament.

ⓔ **10/10 marks awarded.** This final paragraph is not strictly required, but if time permits, it is always useful to include some reference to this material.

Question 5 **The courts system and alternatives to courts**

(a) **Claire has been injured in a road traffic accident and wants to claim compensation. Her claim may be settled in court or through the process of negotiation. Outline the courts (including any appeal courts) in which her case could be heard and explain what is meant by negotiation.**

(10 marks)

ⓔ 'Outline' for this question only requires a brief set of facts about the jurisdiction of courts and the 'track allocation' system.

(b) **Discuss the advantages of tribunals.**

(10 marks)

ⓔ The command 'discuss' requires a full explanation of the question topic covering at least three advantages, together with effective use of examples.

A-grade answer

(a) The size of the claim would largely determine which court heard Claire's case. Under the Civil Procedure Rules, claims for under £1,000 for personal injuries will be allocated to the small claims court, claims for up to £25,000 to the fast-track procedure which would be heard by in the County Court, and claims for over £25,000 to the multi-track procedure which, depending on the size of the claim and its legal complexity, will be heard in either the County Court or the High Court. Usually claims over £50,000 will be tried in the High Court.

ⓔ This opening paragraph clearly and accurately explains the three different 'tracks', their financial limits and the courts which deal with them.

Appeals from the first instance court can be made as follows, provided leave to appeal has first been obtained.
From small claims an appeal can be made to a single circuit judge in the County Court; from fast-track cases in the County Court, an appeal lies to a single High Court judge; from multi-track cases in the County Court, to the Court of Appeal (Civil Division) before two Lords-Justice of Appeal, and from the High Court to the Court of Appeal before three Lords-Justice. A final appeal may be made to the Supreme Court, with leave, provided the case raises a point of law of 'general public importance'.

ⓔ Like the opening paragraph, this one deals just as effectively with appeals from each track/court.

Negotiation is a method of alternative dispute resolution which involves the parties themselves and usually will be undertaken by solicitors acting for the parties. If successful, it avoids the need for court action. Negotiation will involve discussions covering issues of liability itself and the amount being claimed in damages under various headings. In this case, assuming liability is not contested, the defendants would try to reduce the value of the claim being made, challenging the validity of medical evidence or the amount being claimed for future loss of earnings.

(e) **10/10 marks awarded.** This section fully explains negotiation.

(b) The first advantage of tribunals when compared to courts is that of speed — cases come before a tribunal much more quickly, and tribunals can often specify the exact date and time when a case will be heard. Tribunals are usually much cheaper because costs are not awarded, and simpler procedures mean that legal representation is not so necessary. They operate much less formally than courts with attempts being made to create a 'user-friendly' environment which is important if individuals are representing themselves.

(e) The opening paragraph deals with the simpler advantages — speed, cost savings and informality.

A further advantage is that of specialisation — tribunal members already have expertise in the relevant subject area, and through sitting on tribunals are able to build up a depth of knowledge of that area that judges in ordinary courts could not hope to match. A good example is the Employment Tribunal which deals with cases of unfair dismissal, redundancy and discrimination where the panel chairman will be a lawyer experienced in employment law sitting with two assessors, one an experienced business manager and the other an experienced trade union official.

Finally, tribunals can be more flexible; although they obviously aim to apply fairly consistent principles, tribunals do not operate strict rules of precedent, so are able to respond more flexibly than courts. Note also that very few of their decisions are formally reported.

(e) **10/10 marks awarded.** These paragraphs explain the issue of expertise much more fully with a good example. Although this is a brief answer, all the key points in the potential content are well described.

Knowledge check answers

1 40–50.

2 It is a bill introduced by a backbench MP. Examples include: Abortion Act 1967, Murder (Abolition of Death Penalty) Act 1965, Marriage Act 1994, Computer Misuse Act 1990.

3 (a) The second reading is the crucial stage.
  (b) The principles of the bill are debated. This is the stage at which a bill is most likely to fail. This hardly ever happens to government bills, but many private members' bills are defeated on the second reading.

4 Five — the most recent being the Hunting Act 2004.

5 Pressure groups are bodies of people with a shared interest in getting the government to change the law. There are two main types: cause groups which campaign on particular issues and interest groups like trade unions.

6 (a) 1965.
  (b) Legislation that has resulted includes: the Law Reform (Year and a Day Rule) Act 1996 and the Contract (Rights of Third Parties) Act 1999.

7 They are orders made by the queen and Privy Council in circumstances where it would be inappropriate or inconvenient for a statutory instrument to be used. Their main use is in emergencies. They are of particular value when Parliament is not sitting.

8 They are regulations and orders made by government ministers dealing with matters in their area of responsibility. They are used to update primary legislation and to fill in detail.

9 Bylaws are regulations made by local authorities and other public bodies and companies. They only have legal effect within the local authority area or in connection with the specific public body or company.

10 This occurs when a public authority has not followed the procedures set out in the enabling Act.

11 This occurs when the delegated legislation goes beyond the powers granted by the enabling Act.

12 Intrinsic aids are things within the Act itself which might be used to help explain the meaning of particular words in the Act.

13 Extrinsic aids are other documents outside the Act, to which judges might refer to help explain the meaning of words in the Act.

14 The literal rule involves giving words their ordinary, natural dictionary meaning and not going beyond this.

15 The narrow application restricts the use to situations where there is more than one meaning to the words. Judges can choose the meaning that makes the most sense. The wider application is that the rule can be used where the words have only one meaning, but taking that meaning would create an absurd or repugnant situation.

16 Judges look for the evil or problem that the Act was designed to put right and try to interpret any words to give effect to the intention that Parliament had.

17 Judges look for the purpose that Parliament had in passing the Act and try to interpret words in accordance with that purpose so that they give effect to the intentions of Parliament.

18 *Ejusdem generis*; *expressio unius*.

19 The Supreme Court which was set up in 2009 to replace the House of Lords.

20 Although the House of Lords was sparing in its use of the Practice Statement, there are a number of examples of its use. One is *R v Shivpuri* which overruled *Anderton v Ryan*.

21 That the Court of Appeal (Civil Division) is not able to overrule its own earlier decisions except in three specific circumstances: if the earlier decision was made *per incuriam* (in error); if there are two conflicting Court of Appeal decisions; and if the Court of Appeal decision conflicts with one in the House of Lords.

22 *Ratio decidendi* means the reasons for the decision and is the part of the judgement that explains the reasoning behind the decision of the court in the particular case.

23 *Obiter dicta* means 'other things said' and refers to parts of a judgement which are not part of the reasons for the decision. For example, the judge may comment on how the law would apply if the facts were different.

24 Persuasive precedent is a decision or statement of an earlier court which can be followed in later cases, but does not have to be. For example, the decision might be that of a court lower in the hierarchy or there might be an *obiter* statement.

25 Because without it judges in later cases would not have the specific statements used in earlier cases which form the precedent and it would be difficult for a system of precedent to function.

26 Distinguishing is where judges in a later case decide not to follow a precedent set in an earlier case because the facts in the second case are sufficiently different and therefore the precedent does not apply.

27 Overruling is where a court decides not to follow a decision made in a lower or same level court. The Supreme Court can overrule its own earlier decisions by using the Practice Statement, but the Court of Appeal has much more limited powers to overrule its earlier decisions.

28 It has a local jurisdiction and deals with most civil actions up to a value of £50,000 including tort, contract and land law cases.

29 The jurisdiction of the divisions of the High Court is as follows:
  - **Queen's Bench Division.** This is the main court and deals with contract and tort cases like negligence.
  - **Family Division.** This hears all kinds of family cases including divorce, adoption and care proceedings.
  - **Chancery Division.** This deals with cases such as partnership or company disputes and disputes over wills or trusts or the sale of land.

30 Legal costs by barristers and solicitors, compounded by delays in negotiation between the parties and bringing the case to trial. Also the costs rule whereby the losing party pays the winner's legal costs.

31 Advantages include:
- compulsory process
- formality of procedures
- appeal process
- legal aid
- law making and development
- enforcement of decision

32 It shows that courts are prepared to penalise litigants who unreasonably refuse to participate in ADR.

33 A barrister or solicitor will be the chairman and there will usually be two other lay members who, although not legally qualified, have expertise in the area of dispute.

34 Because tribunals now handle far more disputes than courts could ever do; they are much quicker and cheaper than courts.

35 Because the procedure is much less formal so legal representation is not so necessary. Tribunals will also hear the case much more quickly than a court could.

36 Because many tribunal cases — tax, welfare benefits, discrimination at work, immigration — involve complex legal issues, and if suing a government department or employer, that party will be legally represented.

37 A clause written into a contract which requires the parties to resolve any dispute arising out of the contract through arbitration, not by suing in court.

38 Advantages include:
- Parties retain more control over arbitration than over a court case.
- The proceedings are held in private.
- Arbitration is usually quicker and cheaper than court proceedings.
- An arbitrator will be an expert in that area.

39 (a) Against sentence, the Court of Appeal can uphold the sentence or reduce it.

  (b) Against conviction, the Court of Appeal can uphold the conviction, quash it or reduce the level of conviction, for example reducing a murder conviction to manslaughter.

40 The potential juror must be on the electoral register, be aged 18–70 and be ordinarily resident in the UK for at least 5 years. The major change introduced in the Criminal Justice Act 2003 was to remove many categories of people who were previously ineligible for jury service, e.g. clergymen, police officers, lawyers and judges.

41 By the prosecution using 'stand by the Crown' challenge; by the defence 'for cause' and by either party using 'challenge to the array'.

42 Aged between 18 and 65, and live or work within the local justice area. Those excluded include police and probation officers, those with certain criminal convictions and undischarged bankrupts.

43 The youth court is less formal than an adult court. It is held in the presence of three magistrates and the justice's clerk. The magistrates concerned in youth courts must have received additional training and there must be a mixed-gender bench. A parent or guardian must be present, and the youth may be accompanied by a legal representative or social worker. Unlike the adult court, the hearing is held in private and the defendant's name is not disclosed to the public unless it is in the public interest.

44 For graduate entry, either a qualifying law degree or the Graduate Diploma in Law (GDL), then passing the Legal Practice Course followed by a 2-year traineeship.

45 Law degree or other degree plus GDL, then joining an Inn of Court, taking the BPTC, being called to the Bar, followed by 12-month pupillage.

46 The main types of legal work performed by legal executives include conveyancing, probate and criminal litigation.

47 Solicitors are able to offer professional legal advice across a wide range of legal problems. If required, solicitors are also able to seek specialist advice from barristers (counsel's opinion) or from specialist solicitors.

48 The disadvantages of conditional fee agreements include:
- They are an inadequate substitute for legal aid in uncertain cases.
- Solicitors may only take on cases they are likely to win.
- The insurance premiums to cover losing are high.
- There may be pressure to settle out of court.
- There may be a conflict of interest between the solicitor and the client.
- There is public uncertainty as to what CFAs are and how the scheme operates.

49 The Courts and Legal Services Act 1990 as amended by the Tribunals, Courts and Enforcement Act 2007 and the Constitutional Reform Act 2005.

50 Candidates apply following advertisements placed by the JAC, providing references. Additional references are requested by the JAC then shortlisted candidates are interviewed by a panel, after which successful candidates are nominated for appointment by the Lord Chancellor.

51 Because the Supreme Court is a court of the UK, not merely of England and Wales. By convention, two members are from Scotland and one from Northern Ireland.

52 Case-management — allocating a case to a particular 'track'; dealing with other pre-trial issues such as discovery of documents and setting a timetable to be followed by the parties.

53 The executive arm, the legislative arm and the judicial arm. In the UK, the government is the executive branch, Parliament is the legislative branch and the judges are the judicial arm.

54 Tenure of office of all superior judges; judicial immunity from suit; immunity from parliamentary criticism.

55 To investigate complaints made against judges and to advise the Lord Chancellor.